WHY WE GET

MAD

How to Use Your Anger for Positive Change

Dr Ryan Martin

WATKINS
1893

This edition first published in the UK and USA in 2021 by
Watkins, an imprint of Watkins Media Limited
Unit 11, Shepperton House
89-93 Shepperton Road
London
N1 3DF

enquiries@watkinspublishing.com

10 9 8 7 6 5 4 3 2

Typeset by Lapiz
Printed and bound in the UK by TJ Books Ltd.

A CIP record for this book is available from the British Library

ISBN: 978-1-78678-445-2 (Paperback)
ISBN: 978-1-78678-475-9 (e-book)

www.watkinspublishing.com

For my wife, Tina, and my mom, Sandy,
both of whom inspire me every day.

CONTENTS

PREFACE

To know me well is to know that I love talking and writing about anger. All emotions, really. From sadness to fear to happiness to anger, I love talking with people about their feelings, hearing their emotion stories, and helping them learn to have a healthier emotional life. In fact, I enjoy it so much that about ten years ago I created a new class called the "Psychology of Emotion." Here, students and I explore the complex relationships between our feelings, our thoughts, and our behaviors. We study the evolutionary history of emotions and work to better understand both differences and similarities across cultures. We talk about when our emotions become a problem, either because we feel them too often or too intensely, not often or intensely enough, or because we engage in dangerous or otherwise problematic behaviors because of them. Most of all, though, in this class, I debunk the myth that emotions are largely negative by exploring the ways that our feelings help us stay safe, repair relationships, protect ourselves, and right wrongs.

Within this course that I love, though, there are three weeks that stand out as being particularly fun for me, and they are the weeks that we focus on anger specifically. During this unit, we talk about the situations that tend to "make us mad," the thoughts we have when we are angry, and how we tend to act when we are angry. We discuss the biology of anger, the role of upbringing and culture in how we experience and express our anger, and the problems that can emerge from poorly managed anger. We also talk about the positives that come from anger when it is managed well.

Both my TED talk from 2019 ("Why we get mad – and why it's healthy") and this book are borne out of that love. I have been researching anger for more than 20 years, since I started graduate school in 1999. In fact, I went to graduate school specifically because I wanted to study anger. As you will see, I grew up around anger in a way that had me constantly thinking about why people get mad and the damage it can cause. In college, I worked at a youth shelter. Many of the kids I worked with there had difficulties managing their anger and it routinely got them into trouble. I wanted to help those kids and others learn to deal more effectively with their anger.

It was in graduate school, though, that I learned that anger was much more complicated and interesting than I first thought. I had grown up thinking anger was almost exclusively bad and we needed to find ways to feel it less often. But those kids at the shelter – they had a lot to be angry about. Most of them were growing up in abject poverty. They were food insecure, had inadequate access to educational opportunities, and many of them had been abused or neglected by their parents or foster parents. The world had treated them unfairly and they were understandably angry.

This book is about helping people develop a healthier relationship with their anger. I view anger management differently than a lot of people. To me, anger is not something we should quell or push away. Our anger-management goals should not be simply to relax or feel less angry. Anger serves an important purpose in our lives and just as it is not healthy to lose control, it is not healthy to ignore our anger either. Instead, I think of anger as a fuel. It energizes us to do the things we need to do. But, as with any fuel, we need to control it and channel it in particular ways.

To communicate all of that, I have organized this book in three main sections. Part one is called "Anger basics" and it serves as an introduction to the emotion of anger. The five chapters there outline what anger is, why people get angry, the types of thoughts we have that lead to anger, the biological underpinnings of anger, and how we perceive angry people differently based on their race or gender. The second part, "When anger goes wrong," outlines some of the primary consequences associated with poorly managed anger. In those four chapters, I describe the somewhat complicated relationship between anger and violence, how anger disrupts relationships, the consequences of anger for physical and mental health, and how anger can lead us to make irrational decisions. Finally, the third part of the book, "Healthy anger," describes how anger can be understood, managed, and used in positive and prosocial ways. Each chapter includes case studies, relevant research, and activities designed to help you relate to your own anger in productive ways.

The activities, toward the end of each chapter, include all the exercises I have done with my students and clients to help them explore why they become angry, how their anger feels, what it is telling them, and how to best manage it. These activities include brief writing exercises, surveys, and ways to rethink anger. These are tools that will help you, not just as you go through the book, but over time as you work toward experiencing healthy anger.

PART ONE
ANGER BASICS

CHAPTER 1

INTRODUCTION TO ANGER

A misunderstood emotion

I routinely find that people do not know or understand what anger is. They think of it as being the same as the violent or hostile behaviors sometimes associated with it. When they read about mass shootings or riots, they say things like "Why is there so much anger in the world?" When they hear about a physical altercation, they respond with "Sounds like someone has an anger problem." Of course, they might be right. Those might be instances of anger. More than that, though, those things are instances of violence, which is fundamentally different from anger. When we read about physical fights, murders, and mass shootings , a better question to ask is: "Why is there so much violence in the world today?". This question is better because perpetrators of mass shootings and domestic violence do not just have anger problems. They might have impulse control problems. They might have power and control issues. They might believe in violence as a reasonable solution to disagreement. There are a host of personality, environmental, and emotional explanations for violence that do not involve anger.

Now, I am not saying that anger is irrelevant in these examples. It likely is relevant. I am saying that these situations involve much more than just anger, and when we focus exclusively on anger, we are missing some other very serious problems. Conversely, anger routinely goes unnoticed in a variety of other circumstances, as it motivates much more than violence, hostility and aggression.

Anger is, pure and simple, an emotion. It is the feeling state that arises in us when we have our goals blocked or when we experience an injustice. Emotions are fundamentally separate from behaviors.* Sadness, fear, anger, joy ... these are all emotions. There are behaviors that correlate with them (such as sadness and crying, avoidance and fear, laughing and joy), but those behaviors are not the same as the emotional state. People sometimes cry when they are happy and laugh when they are scared. Just as they are sometimes aggressive without being angry.

As an emotion, anger does include a *desire* to lash out physically or verbally, but the emotion is distinctly separate from those actual lashing-out behaviors. In other words, even though we may want to express our anger physically, we do not have to. We can engage in a variety of different behaviors when we feel angry, and many of them are not dangerous, bad

---

* Truthfully, psychologists are not in universal agreement on how to define emotions; far from it. In fact, there is one school of thought within psychology, called behaviorism, where many contend that emotions do not exist. Other behaviorists argue that while emotions are real, they should only be the focus of research when we identify and define specific behaviors associated with them. Indeed, a 1946 article titled "A Behaviorist Analysis of Emotion" by V.J. McGill and Livingston Welch indicated "there is a clear advantage in defining emotions, genetically, in terms of present and antecedent stimuli, since these stimuli are observable and can be reproduced in experimental situations" (p. 120). They go on to say that discussions of emotion should avoid any discussion of mental states, the idea being that we should not discuss the internal states unless we can see their impact via external behaviors. I obviously do not agree or this entire book would be about aggression and violence, the most observable behavioral manifestation of anger. That said, this same article defined love as "an activity directed upon a stimulus identified as a responsive satisfier of needs, or a responsive reliever of distress" (p. 104), which made me wish I had been there when V.J. McGill proposed to his wife.

for others, or bad for us. In fact, some of those behaviors are actually good for us.

I am starting this way because I think anger has an unnecessarily bad reputation. Because people have such a difficult time differentiating it from violence, they fail to recognize that it is truly just a feeling state much like sadness, fear, happiness, guilt, and others. When we are scared, we likely want to flee or find another way to avoid the thing we are scared of. But sometimes we express that fear in a different way. Sometimes we suffer through the fear and do the thing we are afraid of anyway. The same can be true of anger. We may want to lash out, but we can do other things when we get mad.

Ultimately, the goal of this book is to help people understand and move toward two things:

- Anger is a normal and often healthy response to a variety of situations.
- Anger can be understood, managed, and used in a way that is healthy, positive, and prosocial.

That being said, I want to be clear from the outset that I know that anger can be bad for people and for those around them. There is no doubt about that. Anger that is frequent, intense, long-lasting, or expressed poorly can cause serious interpersonal, physical, and psychological problems. None of this is lost on me. Far from it. I became interested in the study of anger in the first place because I had seen the consequences of maladaptive anger in my both my personal and professional life.

I am choosing to start the book this way because I do not want people to respond with "But people can get really hurt because of their anger," or "You obviously have never lived with someone who is really angry. It's horrifying." If your gut impulse when you saw the premise of this book was: "But true anger problems can be awful" – please know that you are absolutely correct. Anger can be profoundly disruptive, and can end in destroyed relationships, property damage, legal troubles, substance abuse, domestic violence, mental-health issues, and a variety of other negative consequences. We have decades of research on the topic and that research consistently finds that anger can destroy lives.

Now, I want you to note that I used the word "can" five times in the last two paragraphs. Anger *can* destroy lives. Anger *can* be disruptive. Anger *can* end in destroyed relationships. But it doesn't have to do these things. In fact, anger *can* be used for good. Anger *can* motivate people to solve problems or to create art and write literature. Anger *can* be the fuel that inspires you to confront injustice and create meaningful social change. What matters most is not necessarily how mad you are, but what you do with that anger.

A poorly timed joke

When I was a kid, I filled up my dad's pillowcase with tennis balls. It was April Fool's Day and I thought it would be funny. I went to bed that night having forgotten all about my joke. I was five or six years old and went to bed well before him, so he had not discovered the prank yet. I fell asleep, and I woke up later to having a pillowcase worth of tennis balls dumped on me as I slept. I do not remember him saying anything as he did it. He just dumped about 20 or 30 tennis balls on me and left the room. He must have woken up my older brother who shared a room with me as he did it, and I remember my brother saying something along the lines of, "I don't think he liked your joke."

I laid there in silence, feeling scared, sad, and embarrassed. I had thought he would think it was funny, but obviously I had been terribly wrong. A moment later, the door opened abruptly. I was startled by the noise, but before I could register what was going on, a tennis ball bounced hard off the headboard of my bed. My dad had apparently found one more and had burst into my room and thrown it at me. I suspect he had no intention of actually hitting me with it, but I do think he wanted to scare me. He shut the door, and we never spoke of it again.

The weird thing about this story is that even though I have quite a few examples of him doing things like this, he was not constantly angry. He got angry a lot, and he would regularly scare me with examples like the tennis ball one, but most of the time he was a relatively happy and fun guy. In fact, if he had been angry all the time, I likely would not have tried my tennis balls in the pillowcase joke because I would have known he would not think it was funny. That was actually the difficult part of living with him sometimes. I am fairly certain that there may have been times when he would have gone to bed, discovered my prank and laughed about it. He would have jokingly given me a hard time the next morning. Instead, though, I caught him on an off night, and he got mad. Really really mad.

My dad's anger caused a rift in our relationship that has been present for most of my life.* We spent a lot of time together, but I was never as comfortable around him as I should have been. I spent a lot of time worried he would get mad at me for something. When I got older, I became less worried about him getting mad at me, but still nervous that he would get angry at someone around us. A waiter would make a mistake and my dad might snap at him or another driver would cut him off and my dad would honk and drive up on his bumper, frightening me in the back seat. He once yelled at a gas station attendant while I was checking out, and I had

---

* One of my colleagues, Dr. Illene Cupit, often says "Research is mesearch" to refer to how often psychologists' research interests are deeply entwined with their own personal life story. While I was unable to find any actual published research supporting this claim, most of the psychologists I know can point to how their life experiences led to their research interests. So there you have it; my personal experiences would suggest that personal experiences are important.

to pretend I did not know him. "Some people," the attendant said to me. "Yeah," I responded. "Some people," and then went and got in the car with him, hoping his anger had dissipated.

One thing that troubles me about this now is that I suspect he never really knew how I felt about this. I remember talking about it one time, and like most conversations with my dad about feelings, it was brief. He came to check on me one night after a particularly scary incident in the car where he got into an argument with a pedestrian (I will have a lot more to say about this later).

"Did I scare you today when I yelled at that guy?" he asked.

"Yes," I said.

"I'm sorry about that," he responded.

I should have said more about how I was feeling, but like I said, I was never comfortable enough around him. That was the nature of our relationship and it stemmed almost entirely from how he expressed his anger.

When anger goes wrong

This tendency to damage relationships, knowingly or unknowingly, is one of several broad categories of anger consequences I am going to discuss in this book. People have known for a very long time that anger was associated with a number of obvious consequences. Chronically angry people tend to get into physical and verbal fights, break things, experience a variety of health consequences, and drive dangerously. These types of consequences have been identified by researchers, clinicians, the media, and a host of other people. In fact, one of the first research projects I ever did was to refine a commonly used survey of anger consequences: the aptly named "Anger Consequences Questionnaire."[1] It was a scale that had been used for about ten years, and my advisor, Dr. Eric Dahlen, and I felt it needed an upgrade to the scoring. The new ACQ[2], as we call it, measures five primary types of anger consequences: Aggression, alcohol/drug use, damaged friendships, negative emotions, and self-harm. Truthfully, it has been nearly 15 years since we refined it and it needs another upgrade. As I discuss later on, social media and other forms of online communication have really changed the game when it comes to how we experience and express our anger.

While some consequences of maladaptive anger are obvious and well-known (fights, property damage, health problems), some are less so. Even the consequences outlined above can be more insidious than people often realize. Take damaged relationships as an example; most of us are aware of how anger can lead people to do and say things that hurt others. Someone feels provoked, they do or say something they maybe would not have done or said otherwise, and they harm a relationship. At the same time, as I mentioned with my dad, there is another, likely more common and often unrecognized relationship consequence associated with anger – angry people tend to alienate, annoy, or even scare the people in their lives.

I will have a lot more to say about how anger damages relationships later in the book. Psychologists have generated a lot of research on how anger impacts relationships, and, honestly, a lot of couple's counseling is actually about how couples can better express their anger to manage conflict. At the same time, though, human interactions have become more complicated as technology has advanced and we communicate in new ways. Email, texting, and social media have provided new opportunities and venues to express anger, and those opportunities have led to different types of damaged relationships.

Of course, another of the obvious consequences of anger is violence. Remember, anger can be defined as the emotional desire to lash out. When people act on that desire, they might become violent. They may hit, push, kick, stab, or even shoot the person they are angry with. This can happen among intimate partners, friends, acquaintances, or strangers. But even the relationship between anger and violence is more tenuous and complicated than we often acknowledge. As you know already, anger does not always lead to violence (it rarely does in fact), but the flip side is also true: violence is not always an anger problem. People are violent for a variety of reasons. Sometimes it is rooted in other emotions (such as sadness, fear, jealousy, and others as well). Sometimes it is not emotional at all, in that people are violent for a particular purpose (to take control of people, to make money).* Like anger, violence is a much broader phenomenon than most people realize.

In Part Two of the book, I will go into detail on some of the common problems associated with anger. I will unpack the research on everything from online hostility to road rage to accidental self-injury to cardiovascular and other health problems. You will see how the dangers of road rage are not limited to altercations with other drivers, why social media can so quickly become a vitriolic wasteland, and how to avoid the broad spectrum of health consequences that can emerge from poorly managed anger. I will also show you how the commonly recognized consequences of anger are just the tip of the iceberg. There are plenty of others. People unintentionally damage their property (ever hear of someone throwing their remote at their TV during a football game?). Or, they intentionally damage their property (ever hear of Steven Cowen, who shot his television with a shotgun during *Dancing with the Stars?*)[3]. They use alcohol or other drugs, get depressed or anxious, and more. The consequences of poorly managed anger are vast and significant, and much of this book will

---

* Every semester, I ask my students how many of them hunt. Being in northeastern Wisconsin, about half the hands in the room go up. Then, I ask them "When you are deer hunting, are you mad at the deer?" They laugh, but this is what I mean about aggression and violence sometimes being unrelated to anger. By definition, hunting is unquestionably an act of aggression or violence (it is a behavior with the intent to harm someone or something). So is wartime combat, self-defense, and even certain sports. All of these reflect common instances of aggression or violence where the motivator may not be anger.

be about describing them as a way of understanding what outcomes we need to avoid and how best to avoid them.

How to "manage" our anger

Many people think the solution to maladaptive or problematic anger is to get mad less often. They see these consequences and say things like "Those people just need to relax," or "Life's too short to be angry all the time." That may be true for some of them. They may need to find ways to feel angry less often. For many people, though, the problem is less about how often they get angry and more about how to handle anger when they get mad.

I once attended a seminar on student alcohol use (as a therapist, not because I had alcohol problems). The audience was mostly college students who had experienced some legal consequences as a result of their drinking. I had very low expectations for the talk. I had been to quite a few seminars on the topic, and I was expecting a talk about the dangers of alcohol use and thought it was going to fall on deaf ears. Instead, though, the presenter started things out by explaining that the goal that day was not necessarily to get them to stop drinking, but to get them to make different decisions about how they drink. She explained that whether or not people choose to drink was just one of the decisions they make surrounding alcohol (where, how much, with whom, being some of the others).

I was pleasantly surprised. I had been to seminars like this before and had taken undergraduate and graduate courses on alcohol and other drug use, and no one had taught me to think about drinking this way. Those seminars and classes had been focused on what goes on in the brain when you drink, what the impact was on the rest of the body, and how to help people who want to quit. Other than my college Alcohol and Drug professor giving us a science-backed hangover cure,* we never talked much about what responsible drinking can look like.

I want to do the same thing she did, but with anger. I want to discuss what responsible anger management can look like. There are decisions we can make above and beyond whether or not we get angry, and we can do more than try and find ways to relax when we get angry. In fact, how angry you get when provoked is just one part of a much bigger and more complicated equation.

In this book, we will explore the triggers that lead to your anger, the thoughts you have when you feel provoked, and what you do when you get angry. When we think about our anger this way, we can intervene at any point in the model to address the feelings more effectively. I want to help you take a more proactive role in preparing for those triggers and shaping your thoughts to help you have a more healthy emotional life. I want you to think about anger management more broadly than just how to keep from getting mad or how to relax when you get mad. I want you to understand the complicated patterns between your thoughts, your current mood state, and the provocations that lead to your anger in the first place, how you can regulate that anger once you feel it, and how you can use that anger in positive, productive, and prosocial ways.

---

* He did so in the context of a discussion of gas-station-sold hangover cures, which he explained did not work. When he told us he was going to give us a surefire hangover cure, I was certain he was going to follow-up with "Don't drink too much." But he didn't, he told us to get up two hours before you need to be up for the day (already sort of losing me), take two aspirin for the headache, drink a sprite to settle your stomach and rehydrate, take two vitamin C to replace what you lost, and then go back to bed and sleep until it was time to get up (winning me over again). Most of it is backed by science but I think the vitamin C part has been debunked since then.

CHAPTER 2
WHY WE GET MAD

"I'm going to kill you in your sleep"

My friend Noah is a professional actor. When he is not
performing at various playhouses throughout the Midwest, he
teaches courses on improvisation, introduction to theater, and
voice acting. One of the first things you notice when you meet
Noah is that he is incredibly nice and easy to talk to. He has
interesting things to say, is a good listener, and has a very good
sense of humor. He seems to care deeply about the people
around him and conversations with him often turn to politics
or other issues of justice and fairness.

I wanted to meet with him because a week earlier he shared
a story with me about how he got angry with a coworker
during a performance.* He gave me a relatively brief account,
and it was interesting, but I was mostly struck by how it
ended, which was with him calmly saying to the person he was
angry at, "If this happens tomorrow night, I'm going to kill
you in your sleep."

I wanted to hear more about it so I asked him to sit down
and talk me through it in detail and to let me record him. He
said he would be happy to (as I said, he is really nice and loves
to have interesting conversations). We met in his office, which

---

* People love to tell me their anger stories. It is an occupational hazard of being
an anger researcher.

I found myself surprised by. It was not what I expected it to be. It was a large space, but was mostly empty. The walls had almost nothing on them, but for a few posters that looked like they have been up for a while (probably longer than he had worked there). "So, this is your office?" I said.

"Yeah," he replied with some hesitation, looking around the room with a look of disappointment. "But I share it with some people so I can't really make it my own." His answer explains a lot. He has told me that he finds inspiration in his surroundings, so I would have expected his office to be a bit more inspirational.

I asked him to unpack the story for me in more detail. I warned* him that I was going to "diagram" it for him. Diagraming angry incidents is something I do in my courses on emotion and the workshops I lead on anger management. It is where we break down an angering situation into all the different factors that led to, or exacerbated, the anger. It is something I want to teach you to do, as I think being able to do this is critical to healthy anger management.

He explained that he was in the play *A Tuna Christmas*. His description of the play made it sound like the stuff of my nightmares. Not watching it – that sounds fine – but performing in it sounded horrifying. The cast of the show is just two people, and each of them play eight to ten different roles. This means that there were a number of "quick changes" throughout the show, where he went offstage and had to change costumes, often in less than 30 seconds, before going back on stage.

This was a two-hour play with just two actors voicing all the lines, so a lot to learn. They had two and half weeks for rehearsal. As he put it, "it was stressful as of day one." They had to get "off book" (have it all memorized), figure out how to get in and out of costumes, and develop the eight to ten

---

* Even though people love to tell me their anger stories, they do not always love to hear my thoughts on their anger stories. Hence, the need for a warning …

characters they were playing in just two weeks. There were only a handful of props in this particular production so most actions were mimed. When he picked up an imaginary coffee mug or opened the imaginary oven, he had to remember where to set that coffee mug and to close that oven.* It all requires a lot of technical skill and as he put it: "It is easy to get rattled when things go wrong."

What is most relevant to this story, though, is the quick-change process. These quick changes happened just off stage. There were three changing areas, so they have to remember which one they went to for particular changes, and they had to change outfits – sometimes completely – and often apply wigs. Noah had three different wigs, one for each of the three female characters he was playing. To assist with all of this, there were two "dressers" who were responsible for keeping the spaces organized and making sure Noah had all the parts of the costume he needed. When he exited the stage for a costume change, things were supposed to be set up the way he wanted them. The dressers were there throughout the rehearsals, because for *A Tuna Christmas* getting these changes correct is critical to the success of the production, and they needed time to work together.

At the final dress rehearsal, one of the dressers had made a mistake. It was not the first time this particular dresser had made this mistake. As Noah described it: "My hardest change was into Pearl, the aunt, because she has so many accoutrements: gloves, spectacles, a hat, and a dress. I was counting on him to have that dress ready for me as soon as I went from R.R., who was wearing overalls, a sports coat, a hat, and shoes."

Noah had to come back, take all that off, and get dressed as Pearl. It is his most extensive change with the least amount

---

* I wondered how big a deal this really was. So what if you forget to close the imaginary oven door? But he said that audiences notice when you forget, and he will hear about it later. I am sure he is right. My kids would always notice when I left the imaginary oven door open.

of time to make it. In rehearsal, they had worked that change several times. When he got back there, his dresser had not reset the area for him. "The dress was in a pile on the floor. I didn't know where the shoes were. The cane was on the opposite end of the clothing rack from where it needed to be. The gloves were all balled up from when I had taken them off last time."

He was in such a hurry to get into the dress that he put it on backwards. His dresser was trying to put on earrings while he was putting on the dress. "Get the fuck away from me," Noah said to his dresser, who then backed off. His anger started to build as he struggled with the dress. There was a pearl necklace attached to it that was in his face. He ripped the necklace off the dress, partly in anger and partly in an attempt to get the dress on.

Because it was a dress rehearsal, there was no audience but for the director, a photographer who was taking production photos, and a few other people involved in the production. Noah called hold, feeling like he needed time to get everything together. He looked at his dresser and said, "Get away from me." He then took a breath, got into the costume, and went out to the do the scene. That brought him to the end of the first act, so he had some time to calm down before starting again.

After he finished act one, he went to his dressing room to calm down. He said he was getting more and more upset as he thought about it and it was affecting his concentration. The first thing he did was go to complain to his co-star about it. He said it felt good to verbalize it. He then got into his costume for the next scene so he was fully ready to go and would not be pressed for time again before going out. Then, he sat down and tried to relax. He sipped some water and tried to think about what was important. "And that was the play," he said. He wanted to let the angry incident go and focus on what was ahead of him.

He finished the rehearsal, but said he did not feel right about things the rest of the show because he was so angry. He said: "This feeling of anger had washed over me like a wave, and when the wave receded, I was still wet. It affected my concentration, and I could feel it."

After the show, Noah got out of his costume and took some deep breaths to help him relax. Before he left for the night he wanted to talk to his dresser about what had happened. They were resetting the theater for the next night's performance. He took his dresser away from the group. His dresser kept apologizing, but Noah had heard him apologize enough times and did not want to hear that any more.

"This is what I want to say to you," Noah described it to me:

First of all, I'm sorry that I got angry backstage during that change. You have to appreciate how hard it is to carry a two-hour play of lines in your head when it's just you and another person. There's a lot going on in my dome, and the reason that you and Dana [the other dresser] are so integral to this process, and why you come and bow with us during curtain call, is because you make it so Allan [his co-star] and I don't have to think about costume changes. You make it so we come off into an organized world. That is why we rehearse these things. That is why you should be writing them down. And thinking at all times, 'What's next?' And then start preparing. I don't want to come off stage and think about scene changes. I have too many other things to think about. That's not my job. That's your job. And the reason I got so angry is because I take this very seriously. This is my career. And if I don't perform well, I don't get hired again. It's just a simple as that. That's why I try to be as good as I can be and why I'm pretty insistent that people working with me are also as good as they can be. So I would just like you to know that I like you so much and think you're nice, and outside of this issue, I really think you're the greatest. But if this happens tomorrow night, I'm going to kill you in your sleep.

The dresser laughed when Noah said this last part, and Noah responded "I need you to believe me."*

The "Why we get mad" model

A big part of what I do is study situations like this to better understand why people get mad. In a lot of ways, it is the same thing I did when I was a kid. I spent my childhood wondering why my dad was mad. Of course, it was not academic at the time; it was self-preservation. I needed to know why he was mad because I needed to know if he was mad at me. And if he was mad at me, I needed to make amends or stay away.†

To answer that question, I use a model outlined by Dr. Jerry Deffenbacher in a 1996 book chapter titled "Cognitive-behavioral approaches to anger reduction,"[4]‡ I cover the model in just about every class I teach on emotion and every talk I give on anger. I think it paints the perfect picture for why people get mad, and I think that if everyone understood it and could apply it to the situations they find themselves in, they would have much healthier emotional lives. In fact, I will

---

* Noah made it clear to me that he would not have hurt his dresser or anyone else. This was a very empty threat. However, he meant it when he said "I need you to believe me." Noah did feel like he needed to be believed on this. He was struggling to know what to do to fix this situation and a threat, even an empty one, felt like his best option.

† Evolutionarily speaking, anger provided our human and nonhuman ancestors with a significant advantage for a variety of different reasons. One reason has to do with communication. The facial expressions people and animals make when they are angry (what are sometimes called threat gestures) let the world around them know how to approach them … or just not to approach them.

‡ One of the nerdier things that psychologists do is track their "academic genealogy." It is just as it sounds. We keep track of who our advisor's advisor's advisor was … and so on. We are a young enough science that you only have to go back five or six people to get back to the founders of the field, usually either William James or Wilhelm Wundt. I bring this up because my advisor in graduate school was Dr. Eric Dahlen, and his advisor was Dr. Jerry Deffenbacher, who authored this article (and many other articles). I think that makes him my grand advisor, a description he probably would not appreciate.

have some exercises for you on this as we go along to teach you the best ways to "diagram your anger" using the "Why we get mad" model.

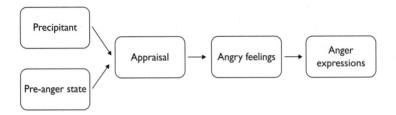

Above: "Why we get mad" model

The precipitant Deffenbacher describes anger as resulting from a "complex interaction" of three things: (1) a precipitant, (2) the person's pre-anger state, and (3) appraisal processes. We'll start with the precipitant or what I like to call the provocation. This is the event that seems to spark the anger. In Noah's case above, the provocation was his dresser not having the space prepared for him. These provocations are often external situations that feel like they cause the anger directly (such as hitting a bunch of red lights on your way to work). It might include the behavior of other people we know (our spouse forgets to put away the milk) or strangers (getting cut off in traffic). It might be a set of circumstances (experiencing significant flight delays on a vacation) or even something that is not directly relevant to you (government policy you disagree with). It might even include something that is largely your fault (you misplace your car keys).

These provocations can even be memories, where something about a situation you are in triggers an angering memory and that memory leads to anger. You see a movie about an office romance, and it reminds you of a previous romantic partner's infidelity. You see a picture on social media of someone you used to work with, and it reminds you of how often you felt disrespected by them at work. These are cases where the anger is not directed at the precipitant, but the precipitant is indirectly leading to anger via these angering memories.*[5]

Or, perhaps it's not a memory but something we think might happen. I was once working with a client who needed to have what she anticipated would be an unpleasant conversation with a colleague at work. She was expecting the worst and envisioning all the things this person might say to her when they talked. She started to get angry just thinking about how the conversation would likely go. When she finally had the conversation, she was primed and ready for it to go badly and had spent a few days fuming over a provocation that had not even happened yet. The conversation went fine, by the way. The person did not say any of the things my client thought they would say and was, ultimately, very positive, making it even more clear that she should not have spent so much time being angry about what might have happened but did not happen.

Ultimately, even though there are some common ones, anything can be a precipitant. When I have asked people for examples of things that "make them mad," they describe everything from big global issues like environmental destruction, sexism, and racism to specific types of people

---

*   Never doubt the intensity of recollected anger. It is very real. In one of my all-time favorite research studies, Dr. Paul Foster and his colleagues compared recollected angering scenarios to imagined and current angering scenarios. They did this by hooking participants up to a heart rate monitor and a measure of skin conductance (which measures sweating) before asking them to either imagine an angering situation or think back to an angering situation from their past. For the third group, after they were hooked up to the measures, they were told that the equipment had malfunctioned and they could not do the experiment. The participants, who were there for class credit, were then told that they would not get the credit for the experiment. The researchers then ignored the participants' questions for a few minutes. As the participants become angry over their mistreatment, the equipment was measuring their sweating and heart rate. What did they find? All three groups became angry, but both the imagined and recollected groups were angrier than the "actual anger" group. Of particular interest here, though, is that just remembering something frustrating that happened to you can actually increase your heart rate and make you sweat.

(such as people with closed minds, deceitful people, bullies).
They give specific examples like buying things at the grocery
store that they later find are passed their expiration date or
when parents do not use the drop-off line correctly at school.
They even mention specific devices or products like sinks that
splash water on you or slow gas pumps.

These examples tend to fall into three broad, overlapping
categories: injustice, poor treatment, and goal-blocking. Some
people get angry when they perceive a lack of fairness in the
world (sexism, racism). Even an example like parents not
using the drop-off line correctly speaks to a lack of fairness
in some way ("Why should you get to break the rules when
the rest of us have to follow them?"). Similarly, most people
become angry over what they perceive as poor treatment from
others. They become angry when they are bullied or when they
encounter dishonesty and disrespect. Related, some people I
talked to became angry on behalf of someone else who was
treated badly. They pointed to examples of service workers
being treated poorly or animal abuse as things that made
them angry. Finally, people become angry when their goals
are blocked or when they are slowed down. You see this in
examples like the drop-off line at school (remember, they are
overlapping categories) or buying expired food ("Great, now I
need to go back and get more milk"). When people are trying
to accomplish something, even when that something is small
and simple, those things that get in the way lead to anger.

The pre-anger state The second piece of Deffenbacher's
model, the pre-anger state, is what is quite relevant when
reflecting on the frustration Noah felt as he was performing.
Those precipitants, or provocations, are made worse when
we are stressed, tired, hungry, too hot or too cold, or in
some other negative state. During the rehearsal, Noah was
feeling stressed about performance. He had the considerable
responsibility of keeping track of the lines and costumes
for multiple parts in a two-person play. He described being
hot and sweaty because of the lights and the physical effort

required to change costumes so often, and he was under a significant time constraint to get into his new costume in time for the next scene. Taken together, he was likely more prone to anger than he normally would have been.

If you think of this situation in terms of both the first two parts of the model, provocation and pre-anger state, it looks like this: he had a goal (to put on a great performance) and his colleague was blocking it. That goal-blocking will naturally lead to increased frustration, but when you add the stress of the pre-anger state to the mix, it ends up exacerbating those feelings. If you were to add additional negative feelings (a poor night's sleep so he is fatigued, missed lunch so he is hungry), you might expect the frustration to be even greater. Even if this had not been the last night of rehearsal, he may have felt less stressed about the status of the performance and reacted differently. The circumstances change and his pre-anger state changes with them.

There are infinite states one could be in prior to the provocation that might increase or decrease one's anger. Some of them could be considered physical states (tired, hungry, physically uncomfortable) and others more psychological states (anxious, stressed, sad, already frustrated). On top of that, what you are doing at the time of the frustration matters too. This is one of the reasons why driving can be such an angering experience for people. The nature of the activity is such that it activates a number of states that predict anger (anxiety, stress, and so on). Along the lines of activities, there is even some evidence that parents who are looking at their phone are more likely to snap at their children than parents who are not looking at their phone.*

---

* Dr. Jenny Radesky and her colleagues did an observation study at fast-food restaurants in 2014 where they watched caregivers eating with children. They kept track of who was using their phone (how often and how long) and how they treated their children. They found that (a) 73% of caregivers used a phone during the meal and (b) those using a phone treated their children more harshly than those not on their phone. In one instance, a caregiver kicked a child under the table, and in another instance a caregiver pushed a child's hand away as the child was trying to lift the caregiver's face away from the device she was looking at. That last sentence is one of the saddest I have ever written.

Appraisal The third piece of this model is the most important part. In Deffenbacher's model, these first two elements, the precipitant and the pre-anger state, feed into an appraisal process. Appraisal is how we evaluate or interpret the different things we experience each and every day. When we face a provocation, whether it is a coworker failing to meet their work responsibilities, a parent failing to use the drop-off line correctly, or being honked at on the road, we must first judge the event and decide what it means. As Deffenbacher describes it:

> Anger increases if the precipitating source is perceived as intentional (i.e., someone or something purposefully directing the event toward the person), preventable (i.e., something that could be controlled), unjustified (i.e., judged as unwarranted and unfair, a violation of a sense of social justice), and/or blameworthy and punishable (i.e., judged as culpable and deserving to suffer).

If we revisit that list of provocations I shared earlier, you see that there is a judgment being made in each of these examples. To be angered by a person with a closed mind, you must first *believe* that closed-mindedness is wrong and *decide* that their behavior reflects closed-mindedness. Both of those are appraisals or interpretations of a person or situation. They both reflect a broader worldview ("People should be open-minded") and a decision about the person in question ("This person is not open-minded"). Those may be accurate and fair interpretations, but they are still interpretations.

Let us use the example of misusing the drop-off line at school. When I talked to the person who voiced this as a common provocation in her life, she said: "You're supposed to drive up, stop the car in one of the drop-off spots, let the kids out, and go. You shouldn't be there longer than about 30 seconds. You shouldn't stop to talk to people, or even get out of your car. And people let their kids out early sometimes too, which you aren't supposed to do, or they spend too long saying goodbye, or they see someone they know and talk to them for a few minutes. All of that slows me down and it's super frustrating."

When you go through that description, there are a lot of statements about how other people *should* behave and what they are *supposed* to do. When I asked her if those were rules that were established by the school and how they enforced them, she said: "They have someone out there encouraging people to be safe and quick, but most of this is just common sense."

So these rules are largely unwritten and are likely not universally accepted or understood. This parent has made decisions about how other parents should act in the drop-off line at school. She is appraising other people's behavior as inappropriate for the situation and is becoming angry when they do not follow the same rules as her. For the record, I largely agree with the rules she has established, and I would likely become angry if I felt people were being rude or taking too long, but that is not the point. The point here is not to judge whether or not her anger is justified. The point is that her anger is stemming from her interpretation of a situation rather than the situation itself.

This tendency to decide how other people *should* act is a pretty common thought type among angry people. Psychologists sometimes refer to this as "other-directed shoulds." The opposite term of course is "self-directed shoulds,"* which is when we make decisions about how we *should* or *should not* act ("I shouldn't have had seconds at dinner," "I should read more"). Not surprisingly, while other-directed shoulds are related to anger, self-directed shoulds are linked to

---

* The often colorful founder of Rational Emotive Behavior Therapy, Dr. Albert Ellis, was fond of the expression "Stop shoulding on yourself" to describe people beating up on themselves in ways that might lead to sadness or depression. He likewise argued that "musterbation" was a similar problem. In the case of anger, though, the issue is too often "shoulding on others."

low self-esteem, guilt, sadness, and depression. There are actually quite a few different thought types that are linked to anger and we are going to go through all of them in a later chapter when we talk more specifically about appraisal and angry thinking.*

Appraisal can be broken up into two categories: primary and secondary. So far, I have mostly focused on primary, which is when we judge the precipitant to determine if anyone did anything wrong. Secondary appraisal, though, is when we decide how bad the situation is and whether we can cope with it. When we decide situations are truly terrible, we get much angrier than we otherwise would. You can evaluate another person as in the wrong (primary appraisal) but end up not getting very angry because you decide that the outcome of the behavior is not that big a deal to you (secondary appraisal). But when you decide that a particular situation is catastrophic and that you just cannot deal with it, you are much more likely to get angry.

If you think about the Noah example above with regard to secondary appraisal, you can see how this exacerbated his anger. The primary appraisal of "He *should* do his job" is made worse by the secondary appraisal of "This is going to ruin the show, and I'm not going to be hired again." If you remove that secondary appraisal, it is still frustrating for him, but the belief that the outcome is going to be catastrophic to the play and his future job prospects makes the situation that much worse.

Of course, appraisals differ from person to person. There is no one correct way to interpret a situation (though, there are probably some incorrect ways) and one person's "This is wrong and terrible" is another person's "I'm disappointed, but it's not the worst thing in the world." When we explore why some people get angrier than others, we find that a lot of it comes down to different appraisal styles. Some are more likely to evaluate situations and other people negatively.

---

* So you *should* keep reading.

They are more likely to blame others when things go wrong. They are more likely to evaluate negative situations as catastrophic and more likely to decide that they simply cannot cope.

Unreasonable reactions

Let me give you one more, much more serious, example. It was the 4th of July and my wife and I were having a small get-together at our apartment. We went to the grocery store early to pick up a few snacks and drinks, including beer. It was around 11:30am and people were coming to our place just after midday so we were a little stretched for time. As I tried to check-out, the cashier said to me, "I'm sorry, but I can't sell you alcohol until noon."

I had forgotten about this particular Mississippi law, which said that you cannot sell alcohol, among other things, before noon on a Sunday. I looked at my watch and saw that it was around 11:45 so I figured I could just wait 15 minutes and buy the beer then. I paid for the rest of my groceries, took them out to the car, and waited 15 minutes to go back in and buy the alcohol. When I went to the check-out, the cashier said again, "I'm sorry, but I can't sell you alcohol until noon."

I said, "Right, but it's 12:05 so we should be fine."

She looked at her register and said, "But the register says it's 11:40."

"OK, but the register is wrong," I replied.

"I know, but it won't let me sell it to you until it says noon."

"That's crazy," I said.

"I know, I'm sorry," she said.

I pleaded my case, but she said there was nothing she could do. The registers were all tied to some corporate clock somewhere and she was unable to change them. The registers were designed to prevent the sale of alcohol until after noon and they could not be overridden. She explained that if I just waited another 15 minutes, I could pay for it and go.

"No," I said. "I'm going across the street to buy it there."

I will admit that my plan to go across the street was sort of dumb. By the time I got to the car, drove across the street, parked, went in and found the beer, it would have been about 15 minutes, and I would not have saved any time. However, it sort of felt like the principled thing to do. I was mad at this particular grocery store (my goals has been blocked by an ill-performing cash register) and I did not want to give them my business.

So we went to the grocery store across the street, got the rest of the stuff for the party and left. We were in a hurry because it was now around 12:20pm and people would be getting to our place around the same time as us. As I was backing out of my parking spot, I saw another car coming down the lane toward us. It was not so close to us that I was cutting them off by backing out, but it was not far away either. Normally, I probably would not have kept pulling out. Normally, I would have waited until they got passed us. But I was in a hurry and felt like it would not be a big deal if I kept backing out.

I was wrong. It was a big deal ... to the other driver at least, because he started flashing his lights and honking to let me know that I was cutting him off.

I want to set the stage here a little bit before I tell you what happened next. This is not to excuse my behavior, but just to explain it within the context of a pre-anger state. I had been having a frustrating morning (blocked goal) where not a lot was going right. The situation at the grocery store was annoying to me and left me feeling a little helpless and irritated. I was feeling tense because I was running late. I was hungry because we were coming up on lunch and I hadn't eaten. I was hot because it was July in Mississippi and I had done multiple trips in and out of grocery stores in the past hour. And I was being provoked by the other driver. When all of these elements came together, I got mad.

So I gave him the finger as I drove passed him. It was not the first time I had given someone the finger on the road. For reasons you will understand in a moment, though, I have not done it since. As I drove off, I looked in my rearview mirror to see that his reverse lights were on and that he was turning around. It was clear he was going to come after us.

"Oh, here we go," I said to my wife.

"What?" she said.

"He's coming after us," I told her, and started to speed up to get away. I certainly did not want to fight anyone. I gave him the finger for the same reason he flashed his lights at me, to let him know that I was mad. I regretted escalating things and did not want this to turn into something more. When I looked again, he had completed his turn around and was coming even faster, and what followed was a short but eventful car chase through the grocery store parking lot and out onto the nearby streets.

The other driver was more willing to break laws than I was. He was driving up over curbs and on to sidewalks to come after me. I was worried not just about my wife and I but about the other people around us. After a few minutes, he managed to get in front of me, driving into the oncoming lane of traffic on my left to cut me off, so I either had to hit his car, drive off the road, or stop. I stopped. He climbed out of his car and ran around the back side of his car toward me. I put my car in reverse and did a backwards U-turn and peeled out as fast as I could. As he was out of his car and his car was facing the other direction, he was not able to get in fast enough to catch up to us.

This entire situation was really upsetting for both my wife and me. It still is. When I think about all the bad things that could have happened, it scares the hell out of me. Had he caught us, he most certainly would have tried to hurt me badly. He was probably just going to try and beat me up, but what if it was even worse than that? What if he had a gun? There are plenty of examples of road rage turning into serious violence and even death. What if this had been one of those?

And that is just the stuff that could have happened to me or my wife. Either he or I could have inadvertently hurt someone else. You cannot speed through a busy parking lot without putting other people in danger. What if we had hit another car? What if we had hit a pedestrian? A billion bad things could have happened in those five minutes and all for the dumbest of reasons; I was in a bad mood, lost my cool when provoked, and gave someone the finger.

Before I go any further, let me just point out how over-the-top this person's response was. I should not have given him the finger, but I never expected that sort of response from him. I bet I have been given the finger on the road about 20 times in my life and I have never even for a moment thought about chasing down the other driver. The other thing I would love to know, is what was going on for him that day. I want to know what his morning had been like. Was he dealing with a similar bunch of relatively minor nuisances that all built up until he snapped? Maybe it was not a series of minor nuisances but a major loss that left him sad, scared, and angry. Does he now sit around regretting his decision to chase after me? Is he thankful I got away because he may have made even worse decisions had he caught me? Or does he still sit around thinking about how great it would have been to catch me and teach me a lesson? I will never find out, but wow do I wish I knew more about how he experienced all this.*

---

* Perspective taking – when we consider situations from another person's point of view – can be a really valuable approach to minimizing interpersonal anger. In fact, a 2007 article by Dr. Philip Mohr and colleagues found that the ability to take another person's perspective into account was negatively related to chronic anger.

ACTIVITY: DIAGRAMING YOUR ANGRY INCIDENT

A good start to better managing your anger is to diagram an angry incident from your own life, by articulating each of these three parts: the precipitant, your pre-anger state, and your appraisal (both primary and secondary). Start by selecting a time when you became angry. Pick something recent enough that you remember well what happened, the mood you were in as it happened, and the thoughts you had.

Precipitant Remember, the precipitant (the provocation) is that event that sparked the anger. People often describe this as the thing that *made them mad.* In this situation, what was the precipitant? Be specific, what was the specific event, situation, or behavior that you were responding to? When you have completed that, take a moment to consider what sort of provocation it was (such as injustice, poor treatment, goal-blocking). Finally, rate the intensity of your anger on a one (not at all angry) to ten (intense rage) scale.

Precipitant	Primary Type (injustice, poor treatment, goal-blocking)	Rating (1–10)

Pre-anger state Now, describe the mood you were in when you experienced the provocation. Were you tired, hungry, stressed, or anxious? Maybe you were already angry about something else, or you were running late for something?

Appraisal Think about the thoughts you had in that moment. What thoughts did you have about the provocation (primary appraisal)? What thoughts did you have about your ability to cope with the provocation (secondary appraisal)? Chances are you did not realize at the time that you were evaluating the situation this way. However, now that you have a chance to look back and think about it, how were you evaluating this event?

Anger response These three elements of the angry experience are all separate from what we actually do when we are angry. I have described several different instances of anger and we have seen several different responses. In one instance, anger led to a calmly worded threat ("I'm going to kill you in your sleep"). In the other, anger led to a provocative bodily expression,* and in another, anger led to a desire to fight and a high-speed car chase through a grocery store parking lot. As we will discuss often in this book, anger can be expressed in a variety of ways. In the situation you are diagraming, how did you respond?

* Which is how giving someone the finger is described in the proposed diagnostic criteria for anger regulation-expression disorder by Drs. DiGiuseppe and Tafrate in their 2007 book *Understanding Anger Disorders*.

So how is anger good for us then?

When we think about examples of anger like the parking lot car chase, it is easy to ask how anger could possibly be good for us. Here I just described an example of how anger almost led to an altercation where people might have been killed. So how can I say with a straight face that anger can be a force for good?

To answer that question, we have to think about why anger exists in the first place. It did not emerge by accident, so how and why did human beings develop this emotional desire to want to lash out when wronged?

CHAPTER 3
ANGRY BIOLOGY

The last time you were good and mad

I want you to think about the last time you were really angry; not just a little angry, but really livid with rage. Think of a time that you were a ten on that one-to-ten rating scale I mentioned before. Maybe you lost control a little bit? Or maybe you did not lose control, but you had to get away from people to avoid doing something you might regret. Diagram the episode using the model we discussed in chapter 2. What was the provocation? What were you doing when it happened and what was your mood like? How did you interpret the provocation? How did those three elements (precipitant, pre-anger state, and appraisal) come together to cause such intense anger?

Now that you have done that, take a moment to think about what happened in your body. Think about what your heart did, what your muscles did, how your stomach felt, and what you could hear and see. Think about each of these body parts and describe how they felt and what they did during the angry episode:

- Heart:
- Muscles:
- Stomach:
- Mouth:
- Face:
- Hands:

I suspect it felt something like the following. Your heart rate was likely elevated, and your muscles probably tensed up. Your face may have gone red, and you started breathing more rapidly. You may have pursed your lips, furrowed your brow, and maybe you even flared your nostrils. If you were really angry, you may have started to shake, and your mouth might have gone dry. At times when people are truly outraged, they will even report tunnel vision, where they lose their peripheral vision and see just what is in front of them. Maybe you have never been so angry that you have felt all of these things at once, but you have probably come close enough at some point (or maybe many points) so that you understand the feelings.

Internal states

We spent chapter 2 talking mostly about the story happening outside of your body when you get angry. At the same time, there is a fascinating story happening inside your body. It starts the moment you take in a bit of information that you judge to be anger-inducing. That information comes in through your senses, usually your eyes and ears. You see a person cut in front of you in line or you hear a person call you a derogatory name. That information is received by a small, almond-shaped structure deep inside your brain called your amygdala.*

Amygdala The amygdala is often likened to an emotional computer deep inside your brain. Like a computer, it processes data from the outside world and initiates emotional responses. Although they are often discussed singularly, there are actually two amygdalae, one on each side of the brain, and some research suggests that they might initiate different

---

* It is the almond shape that gives it its name, in fact, as amygdala is Latin for almond. Similarly, a neighboring structure of the amygdala is the hippocampus, named for its similar appearance to a seahorse (hippocampus is Latin for seahorse). I have seen brain autopsies before and, honestly, I do not see the resemblance. The woman standing next to me did, though, as evidenced by her shouting "Hot damn, that does look like a seahorse!"

types of emotional response, with the left amygdala initiating positive emotions and the right initiating negative emotions like fear and sadness.[6]

They do this research by quite literally inserting an electrode into the amygdalae of a human, stimulating them, and observing the responses. This approach has been used not just for research, but also for treatment. In one famous example, sometimes referred to as "the case of Julia," Dr. Vernon Mark both assessed and treated Julia's (not her real name) violent impulses through such an approach. Julia had suffered from encephalitis when she was an infant and began having seizures a few years later. She was 21 years old when Dr. Mark started working with her, and she had physically attacked people on more than 12 separate occasions. In one instance, she stabbed a stranger who bumped up against her at a movie theater. They had tried multiple treatments including medication and electroshock therapy, and nothing had worked.

Dr. Mark believed that the source of the problem was related to her amygdala, and as described in a 1973 article in the *New York Times*, "Through tiny holes drilled into Julia's skull, Mark implanted electrodes in her brain. The hair-like wires made it possible to continuously monitor electrical signals from her brain and to send bursts of stimulating current into the amygdala." Julia was playing the guitar one day, the electrical signals from her brain being monitored, when she suddenly "bared her teeth, her face contorted in anger and she smashed the guitar to bits against the wall." As this outburst happened, her brain – specifically, the region around her amygdala – had sent out a flurry of electrical activity consistent with seizure.

That was not the only evidence Dr. Mark had, though. He was actually able to produce the same violent outbursts by sending "bursts of stimulating current into the amygdala." Essentially, Dr. Mark was able to replicate those same violent outbursts by stimulating the amygdala. Prior to this case there had been anecdotal evidence that violence was linked to some forms of epilepsy, but this was the first time that link had been established via a formal study like this.

What also makes this case noteworthy is that Dr. Mark was able to address Julia's violent outburst via psychosurgery. After identifying the source of her violent outbursts to be seizures occurring near her right amygdala, he removed a small section of her amygdala. The outcome? Julia had fewer epileptic seizures and no violent outbursts during the next five years while she was being monitored.

So what do these emotional computers do upon receiving and processing this information? Upon determining that you should get scared, sad, or in this case … mad, they send messages to a number of other structures in the brain and set off a cascade of physiological and behavioral responses. One of the structures they communicate with is their neighbor, the hypothalamus, a small structure at the bottom of the brain.

Hypothalamus The hypothalamus is often described as a pea-shaped* structure at the base of the brain. It is the part of your brain responsible for maintaining "homeostasis." By and large, the hypothalamus helps keep you comfortable. It regulates your body temperature, controls your hunger, and controls other daily rhythms related to sleep, blood pressure, and so on. What matters most here is that it helps regulate your emotional responses, because it controls your autonomic nervous system.

You likely remember some of this from high school human biology courses, but as a brief refresher, your autonomic nervous system has two primary branches: parasympathetic (rest and digest) and sympathetic (fight or flight). When your amygdalae trigger an emotional response, they send messages to your hypothalamus, which activates your fight or flight

---

* Which made me wonder – given the naming system we have discussed so far – why it was called the hypothalamus instead of the "cicer," which is Latin for pea. Turns out, it is because it is under the thalamus (hypo means "under"). Thalamus, meanwhile, means "chamber" so presumably the thalamus looks like a chamber?

response. Your hypothalamus is essentially telling the rest of your body to shift its focus from standard operating procedures (homeostasis) to defensive measures. It is saying: "Whoa, there is a crisis brewing. Let's deal with it!"

Fight or flight This is the point in the story when you start to feel the anger physically in your body. Your hypothalamus has now triggered a number of other brain structures to release hormones that will boost your energy. Adrenaline floods the system to increase your heart rate, breathing, and the blood flow to your muscles. This is one of the mechanisms your body has to help you respond to a threat or injustice. By increasing your breathing and heart rate, oxygen and glucose (sugar) get to your muscles faster and you are able to move more quickly and with greater energy and strength. This is also why your face might turn red. The increased blood flow to your extremities means more blood to the face.

Simultaneously, your muscles tense up to prepare for action. We often notice that tension over time, in that chronic anger can lead to some fairly serious muscle-associated pain. In the moment, though, we might shake and tremble, especially in our hands. That shakiness comes from fight-or-flight-related muscle tension and excess energy. All of this additional work that your body is doing generates heat too, so you might start to sweat as a way of cooling yourself in those angry moments.

Our digestive system slows down during the physiological response to anger too. While this goes largely unnoticed by people, there is one part that does seem to stand out, and it is when our mouths go dry – salivation is one of the first steps of digestion. When we are in a state of crisis, digestion is not something our brain considers critical so our energy is diverted elsewhere. Our digestive system slows down as our blood flows to our muscles. Your stomach stops secreting digestive enzymes and the muscles of your intestines stop pulsing to discontinue pushing food through your system.

What is extraordinary is how quickly this all happens. In a split second, your brain coordinates these different structures and organs to respond and take action.* And this is only what your brain coordinates automatically. Moments later, you start to make intentional choices about what to do with that anger, and that all happens in an entirely different part of the brain, called the prefrontal cortex.

The prefrontal cortex

Directly behind the forehead, lies the part of the brain that many say makes us most human. It is called the prefrontal cortex and is involved in planning, decision-making, social behavior, and other advanced cognitive tasks that psychologists often refer to as "executive function." It is this structure that is most directly associated with the expression, control, and even suppression of anger. When you are provoked, you feel the physical feelings of anger immediately, but your prefrontal cortex is where you decide what to do with that anger.

Sadly, much of what we know about the prefrontal cortex has been learned through accounts of injuries. Take, for example, the infamous case of the 25-year-old construction foreman, Phineas Gage, who suffered a gruesome head injury on the job. Gage was involved in blasting away rock to make room for a railroad when there was an accident. An explosion caused a tamping iron to launch out of a blast hole and toward his face. A tamping iron is used to pack explosive powder into a blast hole and this particular iron was more than three foot long and one inch in diameter with a pointed end. The pointed end entered his face just below his left cheek, went behind his left eye, and exited out the top of his head. It launched with such force that this three-foot iron bar exited the top of his head, flew through the air, and landed more than 80 feet away from him.

---

* It takes far longer – about 20 minutes – to return from this energized state, which is something we will spend some time on later when we talk about the physical health consequences of chronic anger.

As ghastly as this all is, the truly shocking part comes next. Somehow, Gage survived. Not only did he survive but was he was talking within a few minutes of the accident and walking without help less than an hour later when he got to the doctor.* He was hospitalized for just over two months before returning to his home.

Gage's story is taught in just about every introductory psychology course in the world. A case like this allows psychologists to evaluate something we cannot under normal circumstances: How people change as a result of significant damage to the brain. What Harlow and others noted with Gage was a considerable change in the way he behaved after the accident. Prior to the accident, Gage was well-liked and hard working. He was considered disciplined and responsible, likely why he was given such important responsibilities at his job. After the accident, though, he was described as fitful, profane, irreverent, impatient, obstinate, and (my favorite) "capricious and vacillating."

Interestingly, Gage's case is often discussed in terms of the personality changes that occurred due to the injury. But I would argue that while, yes, these are changes in personality, they are more specifically related to Gage's capacity for emotional control. Even more specifically than that, his capacity for anger control. Fitful, profane, impatient; these are terms you would use to describe someone with an anger problem.

This has been confirmed via more formal research as well, with studies of children and adults with damage to their

---

* Dr. John M. Harlow evaluated him after the accident and wrote about it in the aptly titled 1868 article "Recovery from the Passage of an Iron Bar Through the Head." The article includes such delightful phrases as "there began an abundant fœtid, sanious discharge from the head with particles of brain intermingled" and "on that day a metallic probe was passed into the opening in the top of the head, and down until it reached the base of the skull." There is no rationale for why Harlow needed to poke Gage's brain with a metal probe. Honestly, it reads like he was just messing with him.

prefrontal cortex showing disruption in their capacity to understand and manage their anger.[7] Damage to this part of the brain can happen as the result of brain surgery, head injuries (car and bike accidents are relatively common sources given that the forehead is so often the location of impact), or even substance abuse. When it happens, researchers can explore the impact on decision-making, emotional control, and response to conflict. They consistently find that damage to this area leads to difficulty controlling emotions and managing conflict.

The angry face

Take your phone out for a moment and find the anger emoji in whatever text or social media app you most often use. Depending on the app, it can look a few different ways, but they share some general similarities (reddish coloring, inward slanted eyebrows, narrow mouth). Now, think back if you can to the first time you ever saw an anger emoji. You likely did not need to be told it meant anger. You just knew from the way it looked. In fact, before the modern versions of emoji, people would simply type >:-(or -_- to indicate anger. That second one is exceedingly simple. It is nothing more than three lines (hyphen, underscore, hyphen) put together to approximate the look of a face, yet people can recognize the basic emotional tone of those three lines without much prompting. It is actually rather fascinating that we so readily recognize these images as anger without any prompting or learning, and it is worth considering why. What is it about these few lines that make it so clearly a depiction of anger?

As they send messages to the hypothalamus, your amygdalae are also sending messages to a group of neurons in the brain stem. These neurons, collectively called the facial motor nucleus, control the facial expressions we make when we emote. Those facial expression are relatively universal – we see a fair amount of similarity across cultures. Starting at the top, an angry person will open their eyes wider, and force their eyebrows down toward the middle resulting in the infamous "furrowed brow" people so often associate with stress and worry. The eyes may bulge or form a hard stare. The nostrils will flare and the lips will either purse with the corners down or open wider to form a square shape with the teeth exposed. Meanwhile, the jaw may clench or jut out forward.

In 1987, an emotion researcher named Dr. Paul Ekman and his colleagues[8] did an extraordinary study looking at the universality of emotional expressions. He asked more than 500 participants from 10 different countries to view 18 different photos of people expressing specific emotions (happiness, surprise, sadness, fear, disgust, and anger). The participants were asked to rate each face regarding how much of each of those six emotions was present in the photo. What Ekman found was that regardless of country, participants recognized the emotion intended in the picture the vast majority of the time. In other words, when the person in the picture was trying to display anger, it was almost always recognized as anger regardless of where the observer lived and was raised.

This is a really important finding in the grand scheme of emotion research that ties back to the overall theme of this book, that anger is good for you as long as you understand, manage, and use it in healthy ways. Essentially, what Ekman found was a universality of emotional expression across cultures. If human beings from across the planet express their anger in essentially the same way, it speaks to an innate expression style. And if it is built in, it probably means that it served an evolutionary purpose.

Think about it this way. If emotional expressions were learned exclusively or primarily from our caregivers, we would see vast differences across cultures. How anger is expressed in Australia would be considerably different than how anger is expressed in North America. But it does not work that way. We see that anger, along with other basic emotions like fear, sadness, and joy, are readily recognized across cultures, even across cultures that have had little to no contact with one another.

None of this is intended to minimize the idea that cultural differences exist with regard to emotional expression. They definitely do. However, those differences tend to be minimizations or exaggerations of these innate expressions (how long one holds a smile in Japan may differ from how long one holds a smile in the United States). In 1990, Dr. David Matsumoto tested this idea by asking participants from Japan and the United States to rate the appropriateness of different emotional expressions in different social situations. Participants were shown photos of emotional expressions and asked how appropriate it would be to express those emotions if they were alone, in public, with family, and so on. He found that Japanese and American participants differed from one another as to how appropriate it was to express emotions in different settings. Japanese participants, for example, found it more appropriate to express anger with people of a lower-status than American participants did.

We refer to these different expectations regarding emotional expression as "display rules" and we learn them from our caregivers and our peers. The expression I make when I am mad is innate, but when I show it, how long I show it, and who I show it to is going to be rooted in the display rules I learned from my parents. If your mom or dad yelled and screamed when they were mad, it is likely that you will too. Some of it happens through modeling, in that we learn through observing how our role models express their anger. Sometimes, though, it happens through more direct rewards and punishments. When kids get what they want by hitting, they learn to hit. When they are rewarded for holding it in, they learn to suppress.

Facial expressions of anger, however, are not always voluntary. Far from it. Imagine, for example, that you are in a meeting with your boss, and someone says something that angers you. You get angry but because your boss is there, you feel the need to hide that anger. Chances are, before you are able to get that anger under control, there is a brief moment when your face will betray you and your anger will be visible to everyone in the meeting. This reflects the difference between voluntary emotional expressions (which are controlled by your primary motor cortex) and involuntary emotional expressions (which are controlled by a subcortical system)*. When you are provoked, those structures deep in your brain initiate the facial response immediately before you can override it with an intentional emotional response. Quickly, though, your primary motor cortex, a structure in the frontal lobe of your brain, takes over and initiates the intentional expression, which may be consistent or inconsistent with how you are actually feeling.[†]

The angry posture

As it turns out, we do not just express our emotions with our faces, but with our entire body by taking on a particular posture. This posture, along with the facial expression of anger, helps communicate to others that we are angry, an important function of emotion. It does more than that, though. The posture also seems to communicate to us that we are angry.

As convoluted as that sounds, consider this example. In a course I teach called "Psychology of Emotion," I ask students to adopt the physical position and facial expressions of particular emotions (anger, sadness, fear, and happiness) to see how they feel. I give them the following instructions for anger:

---

[*] This helps explain the fakeness of artificial smiles in photos. It is a skill to intentionally replicate a real, joy-induced smile, and some of us just do not have that skill.

[†] These immediate facial expressions are called "micro-expressions" and paying attention to them is one of the ways that Dr. Paul Ekman suggests you use to know when people are being dishonest. The micro-expression reveals the person's true feelings while the latter expression conveys what they want you to think.

Push your eyebrows together and down. Clench your teeth tightly and push your lips together. Put your feet flat on the floor directly below your knees, and put your forearms and elbows on the arms of the chair. Now clench your fists tightly, and lean your upper body slightly forward.*

Given the nature of the course, it is pretty obvious to them why I am asking them to do this and what the expected outcome is. Yet, they routinely tell me that adopting that posture leads them to feel, ever so slightly, the emotions consistent with that posture. When I instruct them to – "Raise your eyebrows, and open your eyes wide. Move your whole head back, so that your chin is tucked in a little, and let your mouth relax and hang open a little" – they report fear. When I tell them to "Push the corners of your mouth up and back, letting your mouth open a little" – they report happiness.

These instructions come from a 1999 article titled "Separate and combined effects of facial expressions and bodily postures on emotional feelings."[9] The authors were trying to determine whether adopting facial expressions and body postures of particular feeling states (anger, sadness, fear, and happiness) would lead to participants actually experiencing the target emotions, whether if you put on a happy face you would start feeling happy. Moreover, they wanted to explore posture and facial expression separately (angry face on its own, angry posture on its own, angry face and posture together). They found that for anger at least, each of these conditions (face alone, posture alone, and both together) led to feelings of anger with both together leading to the most intense anger.

---

* It is more than a little disconcerting to look out at a room full of students who have been instructed to glare at you with rage.

Piecing this story together

If we connect these different elements, it looks like this. We notice a provocation and our amygdalae react by stimulating the hypothalamus and the facial motor nucleus. In less than a second, our hypothalamus orchestrates a coordinated physiological response to respond to the provocation. Meanwhile, our facial motor nucleus directs the muscles of the face to make an angry expression. At this point, still less than a second after the provocation, the messages get to our prefrontal cortex which is when we start to make decisions about how to respond. Do we choose to express that anger physically? Verbally? Do we suppress our anger and keep the peace? Do we take deep breaths to try and speed up the return to our relaxed state? What facial expression and posture do we take now that we have control again? These are complicated questions and we need to interpret a number of contextual clues to answer them.

Evolutionary value of emotion

When we think about all of these different physiological components of the anger experience, they speak to a critical fact about anger. Like all emotions, anger exists in us because it offered our human and nonhuman ancestors a survival benefit. These brain structures, facial expressions, and body postures did not happen by accident. They happened through hundreds of millions of years of our ancestors surviving hostile forces of nature.

In fact, Charles Darwin commented on such expressions in his 1872 book, *The Expression of the Emotions in Man and Animals*. Here, Darwin made the argument that we see notable similarities in how animals and humans express various emotions, including anger. He described how dogs, when hostile, will show their teeth and how the hair on the dog's back will stand on end. Similarly, cats will try to take on a more formidable size by arching their backs. When it comes to our closest relatives, the primates, Darwin described how the faces of some monkeys will redden when angry, how some will glare ferociously at a provoker, and how some will purse their lips or show their teeth when angry. Likewise, he even described how some baboons will, in a fit of rage, pound on the ground with their hands and compared it to how humans might pound on a table when angry.

Three benefits of anger

Anger does three things for you that were critical to your evolutionary history, and now serve you in other ways:

1 Anger alerts you to injustice.
2 Anger energizes you to confront injustice.
3 Anger communicates your status to others.

Alerting you to injustice The amygdala, that emotional computer that takes in information and initiates the anger response, has some of the deepest evolutionary roots of the structures in the brain. That is because it offered early creatures the survival benefit of alerting them to danger via fear and injustice via anger. When your amygdalae send out those signals to get angry to the other nearby and also very old structures of the brain, it is one of the ways your brain communicates that you are being mistreated.

Essentially, you are being alerted to a problem in your surroundings. When I talk about this in class, and students are frantically taking notes and not looking my direction, I will pound loudly on my desk to startle them. They react predictably. Some jump and others will even gasp. They all look in my direction, forgetting about the notes they were taking. While it is fear rather than anger in this case, it illustrates the survival benefit offered by the amygdalae. When you notice a potential danger or injustice, you drop everything you are doing to pay attention to the threat or problem. The notes they are taking no longer matter because they may be in danger or under attack.

Energizing you to confront injustice As importantly, when your hypothalamus – another very old structure of the brain – initiates the fight or flight response, it is reallocating your body's energy to confront that injustice or solve that problem. When faced with a provocation like another driver cutting us off, a bad call by an official in a football game, or a person treating us cruelly, our sympathetic nervous system kicks in and our body prepares for a fight. Our heart rate, blood pressure, and breathing increase in order to get oxygen to our extremities, allowing us to exert more effort. Our pupils dilate and our eyes widen to improve our vision, we begin to sweat in order to cool ourselves off and our body shuts down the non-essential organs in our digestive system in order to preserve energy. We now have the energy in the right places to fight that injustice or solve that problem.

Communicating your angry feelings Emotional communication, which happens via our facial expressions and body posture, are similarly critical to human and animal survival. When we make an angry face or assume an angry posture, we are letting people around us know how to approach us. This was recognized by Darwin who pointed out that most species will try to take on a more formidable size when provoked, presumably to attempt to instill fear in their enemies. In dogs and cats, it might be hair raising and back arching. In bears, we see that they will stand on their hind legs and put their front legs up in the air. Even birds will try to make themselves look bigger by ruffling their feathers.

Such postures and facial expressions are important communication tools because they can stop a fight before it starts. In animals, we often call these behaviors, particularly the angry facial features (showing teeth, glaring), threat gestures. When we glare at people or purse our lips, we are letting people know to approach us with caution. We are sending a very clear message that we are mad – maybe at them – and they should be careful how they interact with us.

Even more subtly than this, those micro-expressions of anger can communicate to a child or a spouse that something they did was cruel or hurtful. It is a way of saying, without words, "Please do not do that again." I remember, for example, often trying to read my father's face. Around the dinner table or when he came home from work, I needed to know if he was angry because I needed to know how to approach him. If he was mad – at me or at someone else – I would know not to interact with him for a while and to give him space. I learned that those were not good times for jokes or silliness. His anger was adaptive to him (not necessarily to me or to our relationship), because it meant people would leave him alone when he did not want to be bothered.

ACTIVITY: REDIAGRAMING THAT ANGRY INCIDENT

For this activity, let us revisit the same angry incident you diagramed in the last chapter. Only this time, focus on three specific questions:

1 How did your anger alert you to an injustice? In what ways did your mind/body communicate to you that you had been treated badly?

2 What was the experience of anger like in your body? How did you feel physically and how did this help or hurt you in responding to the injustice?

3 How did you communicate that anger both verbally and nonverbally, including your posture, intentional and unintentional facial expressions?

The exceedingly complicated activities of the brain

This coordinated physiological and behavioral response is really quite extraordinary. When you think about all the structures that are involved and how quickly it all happens, it is really quite phenomenal. Yet at the same time, our brain is involved in another complicated and even more mysterious process. It is thinking about and interpreting the provocation. It is trying to make sense of what happened and deciding why it happened, who is responsible, and how bad it is.

CHAPTER 4

ANGRY THINKING

Sit back and relax

On 31 January 2020, Wendi Williams boarded an American Airlines flight from New Orleans, LA, to Charlotte, NC. She is a teacher and was returning home from a work trip after a teaching conference. It is a relatively short flight – less than two hours – but when given the opportunity to sit back and relax, she took it, reclining her seat. She had no idea that doing so would set off a chain of events that would lead to a massive internet debate about flight etiquette.

If you are not familiar with Wendi's story, here is a recap.* The man sitting behind her (currently unidentified) was in the last row and therefore was unable to recline his seat. According to one of Wendi's tweets, he asked her "with attitude" to put her seat back up during the meal. She did what he asked but after the meal, she reclined her seat again. He became angry at this (again, according to her tweet) and started "hammering away" at her seat at this point, punching the back of her seat about nine times. She started recording the interaction from her phone. In the video, which is about 45 seconds long, he

---

* I am piecing this story together from a variety of articles that have been written about it and tweets from Wendi Williams about the incident. It is quite possible that the version of the story I have put forward is not exactly what happened. The good news here is that the details are less important than the bigger picture and overall response to the event.

can be seen tapping the back of the seat – not hard enough to hurt her, but hard enough to be irritating – repeatedly with his fist. At one point he leans forward and says something to her, but it is unclear what, and he continues to tap the back of her seat. She claims he had been punching it harder earlier, but stopped once she started recording the incident.

She released the video via Twitter a few weeks later and an internet storm formed almost immediately. An online debate ensued over when it is okay to put your seat back, whether he behaved appropriately, and even over whether or not she was telling the truth. The behavior of the flight attendant who intervened was called into question and discussions have started as to whether the flight attendant should be fired, and whether Wendi should press charges. Meanwhile, think pieces have emerged related to the lack of civility in modern society and multiple guides have been written about when it is okay to put your seat back. The CEO of Delta, Ed Bastian, even weighed in with: "I think the proper thing to do is, if you're going to recline into somebody, that you ask if it's OK first and then you do it."*

I immediately became interested in this story not so much because of the debate that followed it, but because of the angry response from the man sitting behind Wendi. Assuming the account I have read is accurate, there is a really interesting cognitive phenomenon at play here, that he and many others who have chimed in on this incident seem to be following, and it is the expectation that others will follow the same *unwritten rules* as them.

I say "unwritten rules" because, to my knowledge, there is no point when an airline customer is told not to recline his or her seat. In fact, my experience has been that the airlines actively encourage reclining with statements like "Sit back, relax, and enjoy the flight" and making a point of telling you when it is okay to recline your seat and when you need to put

* Do you think the CEO of Delta flies economy class?

it back up. This rule then, that people should not recline their seat, is not something promoted by the airline and – at least based on the fall-out from this – not universally shared. In reading through the online responses to this incident, some people seem to think it is fine to recline and others think it is rude. Based on the three guides to airplane reclining I have read this morning, some apply a complicated algorithm to all this which says that we can recline when the person in front of us reclines, when the person behind us is not too tall, but not during the meal, and only on long flights.

If we were to diagram the angry incident from the perspective of the man seated behind Wendi, it would look like this. The precipitant is relatively simple: Wendi putting her seat back. Though it is hard to say for sure without talking with him, we can speculate a little bit on the pre-anger state. He is on a flight, sitting in economy class, so he may be physically uncomfortable (those seats can be cramped). He might even be anxious about the flight as many people are, and he might also be cued up to feel some other strong emotions that traveling can often lead to.* His appraisal, though, seems pretty clear. He has interpreted her behavior of reclining the seat as rude. He is engaging in the same "other-directed shoulds" we discussed in chapter 2: "Other people should not recline their seats, and she is rude for doing this."

Those other-directed shoulds cause not just his anger at her, but they also influence his behavioral response: the punching of the seat. His interpretation is not just that she should not put her seat back, it is that he should be allowed to punish her for having done so. Essentially, he is saying "Her behavior is wrong, I am correct to be angry, and I have the right to try and stop her." Based on the online response to this, many people agree with him.

---

* The emotion researcher in me loves the airport. There is no better place for emotion watching. Fear of flying, frustration over delays, sadness about saying goodbye, or the joy over going someplace new, there are so many strong emotions experienced there.

I should be extra clear that I am not defending the decision to recline an airplane seat. I had never really thought about it before, and I had no idea that there was an etiquette around this. That actually makes it more interesting to me. There are these unwritten rules floating around, that I have been violating without any knowledge of it. These rules are everywhere. Should you walk or stand still on an escalator? How loud can you talk on your cell phone when you are in a public space? Should you pay with a credit card or is cash okay sometimes? There are strong opinions about some of these rules, and they become anger inducing when people violate them.

Angry thoughts

About 20 years ago, I was in a meeting with my advisor, Dr. Eric Dahlen. I had just finished my master's thesis and it was time to turn our attention to my dissertation. I do not remember what the options were that I was considering, but I am certain I was hoping for relatively simple and straightforward. I had seen a lot of people get bogged down with complicated dissertations that were delaying their graduations. I did not want that to happen to me. I was different than those others in that I truly loved research and planned on continuing to do it after graduation. That said, taking on too big a project could have really negative consequences for my career. The field of psychology is littered with ABDs ("all but dissertation"), and I did not want that to happen to me.

I wanted to do something related to angry thinking, and Eric and I were talking through some possibilities. He said, "The problem is that we don't have any way to measure angry thinking … That's your dissertation. You should develop a survey of angry thoughts."

I panicked a little bit. Survey generation can be tedious and time consuming. It would likely mean some pilot studies, collecting data from a huge number of participants, and using some statistical approaches that I had not learned yet. I laughed nervously at the suggestion and he said, "Seriously … think about it. It would be a significant contribution to the field."

So we did it. We scoured the literature on cognitive appraisal as it relates to anger and identified different types of angry thoughts. We interviewed people about their angry thoughts, wrote survey questions, had experts review them, rewrote those survey questions, and asked experts to review those too. We collected pilot data from hundreds of people to narrow down the pool of questions, and after all of that, we collected data from nearly 400 people on the types of thoughts they have when they get angry. We correlated that data with surveys that measured anger, sadness, and anxiety. We explored the differences between the angriest participants and the least angry participants, and built a final survey called the Angry Cognitions Scale.*

The Angry Cognitions Scale measures five overlapping types of angry thoughts that had been outlined in the research as related to anger: overgeneralizing, demandingness, misattributing causation, catastrophizing, and inflammatory labeling. There are likely some others as well, and we will outline some of those as we go, but these five types stand out as the thoughts angry people have that often lead to increased anger.

Overgeneralizing Have you ever been stopped by a red light and said to yourself, "Why do I *always* hit *every* red light?" Or maybe a coworker forgot to do something and you said, "She *always* does this!" These are examples of overgeneralizing, which is when we describe events in overly broad ways. This type of thought is relatively easy to notice because there are some standard words to look for: always, never, every, nobody.

---

* Although we put a lot of work into the scale itself, we obviously did not put a lot of work into the name of that scale.

Overgeneralizing is linked to anger because you end up taking an isolated incident and responding to it as though it is a pattern. In your mind, it is no longer an isolated instance that is happening at that moment. It has become a longstanding and reoccurring situation. In the examples above, you are no longer being stopped by a single red light that will delay your travels by a few minutes. You have turned this single instance into a series of negative events that perpetually slow you down. You are now consistently made late by red lights and have suffered frequent travel delays as a result. Your colleague did not make a single mistake that cost you additional work. She *always* makes these mistakes, increasing your workload, and exacerbating your suffering.

Demandingness When people put their own wants and desires above the wants and desires of those around them, this is demandingness, which includes those "other-directed shoulds" thoughts we have talked about. When the car in front of them is driving slower than they want to drive, they might respond with, "This person needs to speed up so I can get to work." When they are waiting in line at a store and the person in front of them is taking longer than usual, they might think, "This place needs more staff so I don't have to wait so long."

Demanding thoughts like these lead to anger for relatively obvious reasons. All people have unmet wishes throughout their day. People drive more slowly than we want them to, service workers might take longer than we want, or our coworkers might not focus on the work we want them to focus on. When we experience these unmet wishes and desires, there are a number of ways we can interpret them. We can recognize that the world does not always move at the pace we want it to, or we can elevate those unmet desires beyond a desire and into some sort of mandate.

Assuming that other driver is in fact driving at or around the speed limit, it is not necessarily reasonable to say they *should* be going the speed we want them to drive just because we want them to. Similarly, our coworkers likely have competing job demands and do not necessarily have to focus on the exact work we want them to focus on at the exact time we want them to focus on it. Demandingness often comes down to having some unwritten rules about how people should or should not act, how long things should or should not take, and what we do and do not deserve. When people do not share the same rules with the people they interact with, anger often follows.

Misattributing causation Imagine you are waiting in line somewhere, and someone comes along and cuts in front of you. You can interpret that situation in a number of ways. One possibility is that they just did not see you standing there and it was an accident. Another way is that they absolutely saw you standing there and got in front of you on purpose. You could even follow that thought up with additional thoughts about why they did it on purpose (because you looked weak, for example, and they thought they could take advantage of you, because they think they are more important than you).

When people interpret causation or assign blame incorrectly, we call it misattributing causation, and it is another common type of angry thought. It can actually look a lot of different ways. In the example above, it was an interpretation of *why* someone did something as they did. It could also, though, be where we just blame the wrong person for a mistake. You come home from work, see a puddle of water on the floor, and you blame one of your kids for spilling it and not cleaning it up. That may have been a good guess considering past behavior, but later you find out that it was actually your spouse who made the mess and was just about to clean it up. The anger emerged because of a misattribution of the cause.

It is fairly obvious why this type of thought is so closely associated with anger. If we interpret negative things as being intentionally caused by someone else, of course we are likely to get angry at the perceived perpetrator. What is interesting is how quickly some people are to externalize blame. When people lose their car keys, for example, they might say something like "Where did those car keys go?" It may be subtle but that language externalizes the responsibility onto the car keys for *going somewhere* instead of putting the responsibility where it belongs with something like "Where did I put those car keys?"

Catastrophizing Most of these thought types have been reflective of primary appraisal, when we evaluate the source of the provocation. Catastrophizing, though, is more reflective of secondary appraisal, where we evaluate our ability to cope with the provocation. Just as it sounds, catastrophizing is when we blow things out of proportion or when we label events in highly negative ways. You experience a relatively minor setback, and respond with "Well now the entire day is ruined."

You are driving to work and there is unusually bad traffic. You do not know why (offering an opportunity to misattribute causation), but you do know that the traffic will delay your getting to work. There are many ways you can interpret that delay, though, with regard to what it will mean to your life. One interpretation might be to reflect on how late you will actually be as a result and to consider how that will influence your day. Perhaps it will delay you 20 minutes, which is frustrating to be sure, but not necessarily catastrophic (depending, of course, on what you were planning on doing in those 20 minutes). A more catastrophic response would be to start having thoughts like, "Well now my entire day has been blown up" or "This ruins everything."

This tendency to catastrophize makes it harder for people to feel like they can cope with negative events. When you interpret the outcome of a provocation as catastrophic, you start to feel out of control. You start to feel like the world is out to get you and there is nothing you can do about it.

Inflammatory labeling When we label people or situations in highly negative, inflammatory, or cruel ways, we get angrier than we otherwise would.* When someone gives you the wrong food at a restaurant, you might call them a "total idiot." When a coworker fails to finish a project on time, you might label them as "completely worthless." When you are driving and someone cuts you off, you may call them a "fool." These labels have the effect of increasing the anger we feel in response to negative events because they remove nuance in how we make meaning of these situations.

For example, our coworker probably is not "completely worthless." A much more accurate description of them is likely to be the more nuanced interpretation that they made a mistake or that they became overworked to the point that they could not complete their project on time. That does not remove culpability for the lateness and it does not mean we should not get angry. But, a more accurate interpretation of their work will likely lead to less anger.

It is easy to think that we are labeling them in these negative ways *because* we are angry at them rather than thinking about how the label might influence our anger. Of course, that is likely true. We would not call them a fool if we were not angry at them. The trouble is that once we label that person in the car who cut us off as a fool, we continue to think of them and respond to them that way. This is particularly true when we do not know very much about them. We no longer think of them as a human being who might actually be very smart but just made a mistake. We now think of them as a fool and respond to them accordingly.

---

* It is almost impossible to write about inflammatory labeling without swearing. That said, I decided not to, which means some of the examples sound a bit artificial. If you are like me and are prone to foul language, please insert more colorful language as appropriate ("What an idiot" should become "what a f#@king idiot").

Not necessarily "irrational"

Some refer to thoughts like these as "cognitive distortions" or "irrational beliefs," terms used by well-known cognitive therapists Drs. Aaron Beck and Albert Ellis, respectively. The idea being that part of the reason people get angry (or sad, scared, guilty, and so on) is because they are not seeing and interpreting the world accurately. From the perspective of some cognitive therapists, people experience maladaptive emotions because of they have maladaptive cognitions. If I am being honest, a lot of my early work, including my thesis and dissertation, used this language. It is not entirely fair, though. These thoughts are not necessarily irrational or distorted. Sometimes they are accurate. Sometimes other people are to blame for the problems we face. Sometimes things should work better than they do. Sometimes things really are terrible.

Regardless of the accuracy of thoughts, though, we know that people who regularly think this way are likely to experience anger more often and more intensely. Using the scale Eric and I developed, we found relationships between these types of thoughts and the experience and expression of anger. They got mad more often and expressed that anger in more hostile and aggressive ways.[10] They even had more consequences as a result of their anger like physical and verbal fights, risky driving, or other unpleasant feeling emotions like sadness. Plus, in a later study where we provoked them by asking them to imagine an angering situation, people who had these types of thoughts got angrier and were more likely to have thoughts of revenge.[11]

To really illustrate this, consider the following graph that compares the angriest people we collected data from to the least angry. The solid line reflects those people who report experiencing anger most often and in the most maladaptive ways. The dashed line reflects the opposite of that, those people who rarely get angry.

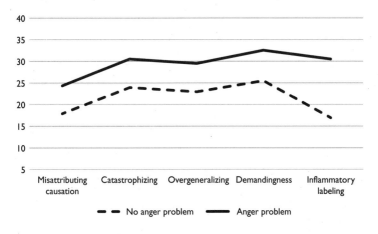

Above: Frequency of thought types based on anger severity

What you see is that the angry group is more likely to misattribute causation, catastrophize, overgeneralize, demand, and label people in an inflammatory way. Now, you might be inclined to think that demandingness is the biggest problem area as it is the highest score of the five types of thoughts. Instead, though, notice the gap between the angry group and the non-angry group for inflammatory labeling. For most of these thought types, the angry group is about five to seven points higher than the non-angry group. But for inflammatory labeling, that gap is 14 points, at least two times greater than the difference for any other thought type. The clear implication here is that while all of these thoughts lead to anger, the tendency to label people negatively is the most dangerous.

"This is your job, not my job"

In chapter 2, I told you about Noah, the actor who got angry with his coworker. When I talked to him, I asked about the thoughts he had when this happened. He broke his thoughts down into two categories: what he was thinking in the moment and what he was thinking later as he mulled over the situation on his drive home. In the moment, he was caught up in thoughts like, "What are you doing?" and "Get away from me." On the drive home, though, when he reflected on things, he had some really important thoughts that helped explain his anger in that moment.

"The first time things go wrong," he said, "I just think, oh well, that's live theater and it washes over me. But I have a thing about mistakes. I don't like to make the same mistake twice, and I definitely don't like people around me to make the same mistake twice. This is your job, not my job. You should be doing this. In general, I don't get exercised about it, but in a situation like that, with those differing pressures, it's harder for me to control myself."

To really understand Noah's appraisal of this situation, we need to move on to later in the story when he takes time to talk to his dresser about what happened. As you may recall, after the rehearsal, he said the following to his dresser:

First of all, I'm sorry that I got angry backstage during that change. You have to appreciate how hard it is to carry a two-hour play of lines in your head when it's just you and another person. There's a lot going on in my dome, and the reason that you and Dana [the other dresser] are so integral to this process, and why you come and bow with us during curtain call, is because you make it so Allan [his co-star] and I don't have to think about costume changes. You make it so we come off into an organized world. That is why we rehearse these things. That is why you should be writing them down. And thinking at all times, 'What's next?' And then start preparing. I don't want to come off stage and think about scene changes. I have too many other things to think about. That's not my job. That's your job. And the reason I got so angry is because I take this very seriously. This is my career. And if I don't perform well, I don't get hired again. It's just a simple as that. That's why I try to be as good as I can be and why I'm pretty insistent that people working with me are also as good as they can be. So I would just like you to know that I like you so much and think you're nice, and outside of this issue, I really think you're the greatest. But if this happens tomorrow night, I'm going to kill you in your sleep.

This interaction tells us a lot about how Noah was appraising this situation. We hear him say the following things:

- You have to appreciate how hard it is to carry a two-hour play of lines in your head.
- That's not my job. That's your job. You should be doing this.
- This is my career. And if I don't perform well, I don't get hired again.
- That's why I try to be as good as I can be and why I'm pretty insistent that people working with me are also as good as they can be.

His interpretation looks like this: "My job is hard to do well. If I do not do it well, the consequences for me are significant. I insist that you do your job well so that I can do my job well." If we were to map out these statements on a scale of one (lowest) to five (highest) with regard to the thought types of the Angry Cognitions Scale, it might look something like this:

- **Overgeneralizing:** 1. We do not see much overgeneralizing articulated here. Overgeneralizing would be something like, "He's always making mistakes" or "He never does this the way I want him to."
- **Demandingness:** 4. There is a fair amount of demandingness in his thought process: "You have to appreciate," "You should be doing this," and "I'm pretty insistent that people working with me are also as good as they can be."

- **Misattributing causation:** 1. This is not relevant in this case. Had he speculated about why his dresser was making mistakes (such as "He's doing this on purpose"), it might be relevant.
- **Catastrophizing:** 5. Noah has definitely interpreted this as relatively catastrophic. By saying things like "If I don't perform well, I don't get hired again," he is indicating that mistakes like this could lead to the end of his career.
- **Inflammatory labeling:** 1. At least on the surface, he is not describing his coworker in really negative ways (he is not using words like "incompetent" or "idiot"). In fact, he said really nice things about him other than this specific incident.

ACTIVITY: MAP OUT YOUR ANGRY THOUGHTS

In previous chapters, you diagramed an angry incident. I want to go back to that incident and focus exclusively on the appraisal process. Take a moment to think about the thoughts you had in that moment (both primary and secondary appraisal). List as many as you can remember.

Now, take a moment to rate the overall series of thoughts from one (not at all) to five (quite a bit) on each of the thought types listed above. In other words, when you read the sequence of thoughts, how much catastrophizing, overgeneralizing, and so on, were you doing? None? Some? Quite a bit?

- **Overgeneralizing:** 1 = None; 2, 3 = Some; 4, 5 = Quite a bit
- **Demandingness:** 1 = None; 2, 3 = Some; 4, 5 = Quite a bit
- **Misattributing causation:** 1 = None; 2, 3 = Some; 4, 5 = Quite a bit

- **Catastrophizing:** 1 = None; 2, 3 = Some; 4, 5 = Quite a bit
- **Inflammatory labeling:** 1 = None; 2, 3 = Some; 4, 5 = Quite a bit

If you would like to see how you compare with others on these thoughts based on the Angry Cognitions Scale, you can do so here: alltheragescience.com/surveys/

Right to be angry

I want to reiterate, I do not know or think that Noah's interpretations are incorrect. I actually think it is totally reasonable to want and expect your colleagues to do their job well and not to make many mistakes. I suspect Noah is correct that a poor performance will make it harder for him to find work in the future. I imagine the acting community is relatively small and the failures have a tendency to echo. This is what I mean when I say that sometimes we are right to be angry.

That said, one clear and consistent finding across the anger research literature is that not everyone gets the same *right to be angry*. While some people may be rewarded and praised for their anger, others are told to be civil, to calm down, and even lose credibility. Before we can fully recognize the pitfalls and positives of anger, we need to recognize that the consequences are not distributed equally.

CHAPTER 5
RACE, GENDER, AND ANGER

"Who gets to be angry?"

A few days after I gave my TED talk ("Why we get mad – and why it's healthy"), I was part of a panel discussion for a group of local activists in Green Bay, Wisconsin. The event was framed around civil discourse on social media. The keynote speaker, a professor of communications at the University of Wisconsin-Oshkosh named Dr. Tony Palmeri, talked about civility broadly, touching nicely on what it means to be civil but also discussing the notion of "the weaponization of civility." He described a scenario where two neighborhoods in the same city have vastly different resources. One neighborhood has plenty of parks and green spaces for kids to play and the other has very few of such spaces. One has beautiful homes and safe neighborhoods and nice schools and the one right next to it has homes and schools that have fallen into disrepair. He said: "Invariably what happens is that people on that side of the tracks get angry and speak up, and at that moment someone from the 'nicer' part says 'We need civility.'... I would plead with all of you to ask yourself *where really is the incivility in that example?*"

We see situations like this happen all too often. A group is systematically and profoundly mistreated and when they respond with any form of anger, be it peaceful or not, they are called on to *be respectful* or *be civil*. To Dr. Palmeri's point, in 2015 and 2016 when Flint Michigan's water was allowed to become toxic, citizens protested loudly and at times aggressively. The Michigan Governor at the time, Rick Snyder (who has since been accused of lying and covering up the crisis in a report published by *VICE*), authored an open letter calling for civility in public debate.[12] A few months later in one of his last speeches before leaving office[13] he described a lack of civility as the greatest threat to the country.* The people of Flint had been poisoned by their government, and were then shamed publicly for not being angry about it in the right way. Meanwhile, as I write this, the United States is embroiled in nation-wide protests of police brutality against African Americans. Social media is exploding with calls for protesters to *be civil* and *calm* and *respectful* and *peaceful* even as they are being attacked by aggressive police officers and threatened publicly by the President of the United States. Again, we see people who have suffered extraordinarily unfair treatment and abuse being told how they *should* express their anger in response.

This is what weaponized civility looks like, and the subtext of both of these examples is race. In both cases we have protesters who are mostly African American and oppressors who are mostly white shaming them for their anger. This too was discussed at that same event as Dr. Palmeri's keynote. During the panel discussion I was a part of that day, when I voiced my position that anger is a healthy response to mistreatment, another panelist named Angela Lang said to me, "Can we talk for a moment about who *gets* to be angry?"

Angela Lang is the Executive Director of Black Leaders Organizing Communities. She described for the audience

---

* I have to believe that the people of Flint thought that the lead in their water was a greater threat.

how her anger as an African American woman is perceived compared to others who work in similar positions to her:

> When I saw my counterparts doing the same, they were assertive. They were aggressive in a good way. Yet, I was an angry black woman in a very negative way. I needed to be silenced. Going back to tone-policing, and civility, and I think something that is also really relevant right now is this hashtag, #takeaknee. Telling people there is a right way to protest. Telling people there is a right way to be angry, which is ironic to have people who are oppressors telling the oppressed community this is how you should deal with your anger. This is a large part of why I don't engage on social media … because I am seen as the angry black woman when I am defending myself or defending my identity or my beliefs, and then that no longer becomes productive because I'm very easily dismissed. She's just angry, so her points aren't valid, and I don't really need to engage with her.

"Who gets to be angry?" is a completely fair question, and frankly, a fair criticism of my TED talk. The argument behind both my talk and this book is that anger is a healthy and powerful force in our lives, and that we should use it as fuel to power us toward meaningful change. Built into that argument, though, is the idea that there are better and worse ways of expressing our anger. I can see how someone would hear my position and interpret it as *there is a right way to be angry.*

To really make the case that anger is a powerful and healthy force in our lives, I want to acknowledge a few things:

1 There is no single *best* way to express anger.
2 Anger expressions are perceived differently based on the gender, race, and other characteristics of the angry person.

3 The consequences of those expressions are very different based on the gender, race, and other characteristics of the angry person.

I did not unpack any of this is my talk. I could have, and maybe I should have. I will not make that mistake again, so I am going to go through these positions now.

No best way

First, there is no single best way to express anger. The best things to do when you are angry are always contextual. It depends on who you are, who you are with, what the circumstances are, what the goals are, and a billion other factors. Arguments that we need to *always* stay calm or *never* yell or even that we *must always* remain peaceful do not get very far with me.* It is of course smart to stay calm at times, but there are times when it makes sense to yell and scream to make sure we are heard. There are also times when suppressing our feelings in the moment is best, maybe because of who we are with or maybe so we can express them in a different way later that is more likely to be successful.

Ultimately, there are infinite ways we can express and use our anger when we are mad. Protesting, organized boycotts, letter-writing campaigns, and petition forming are all viable options. Others choose to channel their anger into poetry, art, or music. Others may choose to remove themselves from a situation because they are scared they cannot stay calm enough to be productive, but later return to voice their anger in a way they are more comfortable with. This is something we will tackle in detail later in the book, but it is important to note right now that *anger management* does not always mean *staying calm*. Far from it. Often, it means *fighting back* against unfairness and injustice.

* You probably know by now how I feel about overgeneralizing like this.

77

Perceptions of anger differ

I have covered appraisal quite a bit so far in the book. It is a hugely influential aspect of why we get angry. A big reason for that is because it is a hugely influential aspect of all human interactions. People interpret the situations they find themselves in based on how they perceive the behavior of the people they are interacting with. They bring to that interpretation their own personal values, ideas, and biases. We can think of this as a lens by which we view the world and it is informed by our learning history. What this of course means in the context of anger is that the race, gender, and age (and other factors) of the angry person matters with regard to how the angry response is perceived. Just as Angela Lang described, not everyone has the same freedom to express their anger.

The research on this is very clear. An extremely impressively designed research project on this came out as recently as 2017 when Dr. Jessica Salerno and her colleagues explored this via a multi-part study.[14] First, they asked participants to indicate the degree to which they recognized and endorsed particular emotional stereotypes (such as: women are more emotional than men, African Americans are more angry than white Americans). They asked 88 research participants if anger and fear were part of the stereotype for both African American and white men and women. They found that white men were more stereotypically angry than white women, and that African American men and women were equally stereotypically angry. And, confirming Lang's argument, African American women were more stereotypically angry than white women.

What this means in the broader context, as stated by the authors, is that "expressing anger confirms stereotypes about black men and black women, but violates stereotypes for white women." In other words, when men, regardless of race, and African American women become angry, they are essentially confirming stereotypes for onlookers. Essentially, as Lang described in her personal experiences, the emotion is more easily written off. When white women become angry, though, it violates the stereotype and appears more unusual than onlookers might expect.

This was just the first part of their study. In part two, though, they were exploring whether women were perceived as less influential when they expressed anger. The methodology here is both complicated and fascinating so bear with me for a moment. To test this, they had 266 participants view a scripted trial simulation via computer about a man charged with murdering his wife (based on a real trial). The research participants served as jurors in the deliberations and read the comments from five other jurors.

The key here is that the research participants did not know the other jurors were fake. They thought they were interacting with other research participants rather than what was actually just scripted text. After reviewing trial evidence, they were asked to provide a verdict and support their verdict with an explanation. They then found that four of the five other jurors agreed with them, but there was one "holdout" who did not. They read the other jurors' comments and repeated the same process again. They did this several times and the holdout continued to disagree with them. Eventually, they were told that the study needed to come to an end because they were running out of time and that there would be no final decision on the trial.

To answer their research question ("Are women who express anger less influential?"), they manipulated the gender of the holdout (by naming them either Jason or Alicia) and the emotionality of the holdout by having them make statements like "Seriously, this just makes me angry/freaks me out." They also added exclamation points and capital letters.* After the deliberations were "cut short" by the experimenter, participants completed a quick survey about the other jurors (ultimately, the real outcome of interest). Here is what they found:

---

* The universal language of text RAGE!

Female holdouts who expressed anger (and fear) were perceived as more emotional and less influential than male holdouts who made the same *exact* comments and expressed the same *exact* emotions. In other words, when men expressed anger, it did not decrease their influence. But when women expressed anger, it did. It is exactly as Lang said during that panel … women do not *get* to be angry in the same way as men.

Dr. Salerno and her colleagues took things one step further with part three of their study. They did the same thing as in the second part, but this time the race of the holdout was manipulated along with gender. They selected what they described as "white" or "black" sounding names. Males were either Logan or Jamal and females were either Emily or Lateisha. They based their decision of what names to select on previous research and pilot analyses.*

What happened in part three? Well, the findings are what we might expect based on the findings from part two. Their participants – 61 per cent of whom were female and only 20 per cent white – regarded African American holdouts (Jamal and Lateisha) as less influential when they got mad whereas white holdouts (Logan and Emily) were not. This happened despite all these holdouts making the exact same arguments and expressing the same anger in the same way. The perceptions of that anger were simply different based on race.

The authors make a statement in their description of these findings that I want to unpack a little bit because they connect to the comments from both Lang and Palmeri. Specifically,

---

* It is worth noting the lengths that this research team went to ensure they did not make any unreasonable assumptions here. They did a pilot analysis to make sure they selected names that really did evoke perceptions of race from participants. Later, they did a manipulation check, where they confirmed that it really did work and participants assumed Logan and Emily were white and that Jamal and Lateisha were black. That is extraordinarily thorough, and it makes it all the more irritating to me that research is so often ignored by the public and policy-makers in favor of anecdotes and personal opinions.

the article states: "Being perceived as emotional might have given people a non-race-related license to discredit African American (but not white) group members' opinions." This suggestion is rooted in what is called the "justification-suppression model of prejudice"[15] whereby people attempt to avoid blatant prejudice yet still end up expressing it when they can find what they regard as justification. People intentionally or unintentionally look for ways to discredit girls, women, people of color, and likely other groups. In this instance, the justification is emotionality, and it is being used to discount the opinions of women and African Americans. They want to avoid blatant prejudice so instead of saying "your opinion is not valuable to me because you are African American/a woman" they say "your opinion is not valuable to me because you are so emotional/angry."

Consequences of anger differ

These differences in perceptions have very real consequences to already marginalized groups. For starters, having your arguments minimized or ignored because you seem angry brings with it obvious negative outcomes. You must work harder and better to "control yourself" than a white man would in order to achieve the same level of influence. Put differently, what that *really* means is that to influence someone in a meaningful way, a woman or person of color must somehow communicate that they do not feel *too* strongly or care *too* much.

We can see this playing out in the United States right now. As people, many of them African American and/or female, protest police brutality, there is a contingent of Americans who claim to support the cause but not the means of protest. Twitter and Facebook are abuzz with people essentially shaming protesters for their behavior, and a recent poll reveals that even though 89 per cent of respondents believe racism is a problem in American society, only 27 per cent think the current protests are justified.[16] America is essentially saying, "We agree that you should be mad, but you should not express your anger this way." It is worth noting that in 2016 when American football player, Colin Kaepernick, protested the very same thing by taking a knee during the national anthem, he was similarly shamed. Polling at the time indicated that the 61% of Americans did not agree him.[17]

But there is also evidence that African Americans and women suffer even more direct consequences as a result of these biases. Take, for example, a 2020 study that found significant racial/ethnic and gender disparities related to how anger management therapy is used as a legal probation condition.[18] The authors looked at data on law offenders from an adult probation department in Texas. They had records for more than 4,000 people, and those records included age, race, gender, nature of the crime, and whether the judge had included anger management as part of their sentence/ probation guidelines. The offenses included violent crimes like assault, but also nonviolent crimes like drug possession, drunk driving, and theft. Because the authors were interested in the rates at which anger management was assigned as a condition of probation regardless of other factors, they used a statistical technique that would *control* for the type of crime, the judge, and the location of the crime.

What they found is troubling. The good news is the type of offense did explain why some people were assigned anger management training. If you committed a violent crime, you were nearly 15 times more likely to get anger management training. That makes sense, and you would likely want that outcome.* Similarly, particular judges were also more likely to assign anger management training. This too is not surprising. You would expect particular judges to have *relatively* consistent sentences.

---

* This is of course assuming anger management training works in these examples, which the jury might still be out on.

The part that is troubling, though, is that even when you control for all those variables, the odds of receiving anger management as a probation condition were nearly twice as high for African Americans than for white offenders. They did not find this difference when they compared white to Hispanic offenders, so the role of race seems unique to African Americans in this study (though the authors are quick to point out that other research has found similarly troubling biases for Hispanic offenders). This discrepancy was even more pronounced when the analyses were broken down by gender with African American women nearly three times as likely as white women to be sentenced to anger management training.

To explain these differences, the authors offer the following: "Our findings may be the result of well-researched findings that racial/ethnic minorities are often viewed by nonminorities as angry, hostile, or threatening." To be clear, these sentences of anger management therapy are not *instead* of other consequences. They are *in addition to* other consequences, so ultimately what is happening here is that being African American brings with it an additional financial (offenders pay for the treatment on their own) consequence due to those stereotypes of "angry black men/women." Finally, to make matters worse, the authors point to very mixed results regarding the success of mandated anger management therapy. The therapy they are being forced to pay for and participate in might not even work for them.

The mental and physical health consequences of racism and sexism

It is important to acknowledge that the consequences of racism, sexism, and other forms of institutionalized discrimination are vast and go well beyond negative financial and legal outcomes. There are considerable mental and physical health consequences as well. Such prejudice and discrimination lead to long-term exposure to the idea that being female and/or nonwhite is "less than," and this brings with it self-esteem issues that are associated with mental-health problems like depression and body-image issues. Similarly, women and nonwhites are more often exposed to legitimate threats to safety (sexual assault, harassment, domestic abuse, police brutality). The daily fears that accompany those threats increase the potential for anxiety disorders.

My friend, former colleague, and health psychologist, Dr. Regan A.R. Gurung, talked about this with me in detail on an episode of my podcast *Psychology and Stuff*. He said: "The bottom line is that discrimination is a stressor. If somebody feels discriminated against – if somebody is repeatedly discriminated against – that is the equivalent of repeated stressors against their body that then show up in all the ways that we normally measure stress."

Since we know that stress impacts our physical health and mental health, those who are the victims of racism, sexism, and other forms of discrimination are undoubtedly suffering physical and mental-health consequences. A 2017 article in the *New York Times* written by Douglas Jacobs[19] argues exactly this and states the following: "More than 700 studies on the link between discrimination and health have been published since 2000. This body of work establishes a connection between discrimination and physical and mental well-being."

In these findings of the physical and mental-health consequences of discrimination, it is likely that the health impact of chronic anger is being ignored, let alone the psychological toll of having your opinions unfairly minimized and delegitimized due to your anger. Unless being discussed as a symptom of some other mental-health problem (such as major depressive disorder, narcissistic personality disorder, antisocial personality disorder), anger is routinely ignored in discussions of mental health. Indeed, chronic anger is not even included as its own disorder in the *Diagnostic and Statistical Manual of Mental Disorders* (*DSM-5*).

Additionally, we have very little information about how anger is perceived in other groups or based on other characteristics. The research presented here has been almost exclusively focused on African Americans and women, but what about other racial groups and ethnicities? What about nonbinary genders? What about age? Might we find that anger is perceived differently when the angry person is elderly? Are people more likely to minimize the anger from teenagers as being rooted in naivety or adolescent hormones rather than real concerns that deserve attention?

There are a host of ways that we may be minimizing the positions of others based on their anger. Quite frankly, while the research can tell us a lot about how this happens generally, it is also likely that all of us have individualized biases that influence how we interpret the anger of others when we are in some sort of conflict disagreement. Part of having a healthier relationship with anger is learning to understand those biases.

ACTIVITY: RECOGNIZING BIASES

This activity is designed to help you consider how your biases might be influencing your interpretation of angering events and interpersonal conflicts. There are three steps:

1 Think back to a recent time when you were in conflict with another person where each of you were angry at each other.
2 Consider how you evaluated the appropriateness of their anger expressions at the time. Did what they said and how they behaved seem appropriate to you at the time? Did you evaluate them negatively because of their anger?

3 Think about whether the lens by which you viewed them influenced your interpretation. In what way did their age, gender, race, socioeconomic status, religion, or any other factor influence how you interpreted their anger?

Revisiting the weaponizing of civility

When I think back to Palmeri's talk and Lang's later question – "Who gets to be angry?" – along with the research presented here and elsewhere, it becomes wholly obvious how civility has been weaponized to minimize the experiences and opinions of already marginalized groups. From mass protests over police brutality to the interactions of jurors to the sentencing of offenders, we see very real and clear examples of how emotionality can be used for discrimination. It is profoundly unjust for a society to systematically oppress groups of people – to create so much to be angry about – and then tell people to remain calm and peaceful and to not show any rage.

At the same time, we know that such anger can be used for good and that how we channel it makes all the difference. Before we talk about how anger can be used in positive and healthy ways, though, we should get into discussions about how and when anger can go wrong in part two.

PART TWO

WHEN ANGER GOES WRONG

CHAPTER 6
VIOLENCE AND IMPULSE CONTROL

"I lost my cool"

On 14 November 2019, nearly 12 million people were watching an American football game between the Pittsburg Steelers and the Cleveland Browns. There were 15 seconds left of the game and the Browns were up by 14 points. It was pretty much over when a scuffle broke out between Myles Garrett, a defensive player for the Browns, and the quarterback for the Steelers, Mason Rudolph. In the middle of that scuffle, Garrett pulled Rudolph's helmet off and swung it at him, hitting him over the head with it. Even in the context of football, an aggressive and often brutal sport, it stood out as particularly vicious incident. In fact, the commentator that night, Troy Aikman, referred to it as "one of the worst things I have ever seen on a football field."

The next day, Garrett issued an apology. He said:

Last night, I made a terrible mistake. I lost my cool and what I did was selfish and unacceptable. I know that we are all responsible for our actions and I can only prove my true character through my actions moving forward. I want to apologize to Mason Rudolph, my teammates, our entire organization, our fans and to the NFL. I know

I have to be accountable for what happened, learn from
my mistake and I fully intend to do so.

Two days later, Garrett was suspended indefinitely without pay.
He missed the final six games of the season, which amounted
to a salary loss of $1,139,911.76. He was also fined more
than $45,000 by the NFL.[20] The NFL reinstated him on 12
February 2020. It's worth noting that on that same play in
response to Garrett's aggression, an offensive lineman for the
Steelers, Maurkice Pouncey, punched Garrett in the head four
times, kicked him in the head one time, and then hit him in
the head again. Pouncey was fined $35,096 and suspended for
two games without pay leading to lost wages of $117,647.05.

There was a massive social media storm in response to all
of this. Twitter erupted with tweets from current and former
players, coaches, commentators, and the general public. Nearly
everyone agreed that Garrett behaved terribly so much of
this online discussion ended up being about *how* terrible it
really was. Some argued it should be considered a crime, some
argued about what the NFL's punishment should be, and some
suggested his career might be over. A few, though, offered
support. Former NFL cornerback, Deion Sanders, tweeted:
"Praying for u brother. It was a quick reaction but it was the
wrong reaction."

I bring this incident up for two reasons. First, it is a great
example of a situation where someone's anger got the best of
them and led to violence. Before that incident, Garrett was not
necessarily known as a dirty player. I know that is a judgment
call by me that people will disagree with, but excluding
offsides and similar penalties that do not have anything to
do with aggression, he had three penalties against him this
season, which is about average for a player at that position.
Two of those were in the same game, which did prompt some
conversation about whether he was an overly aggressive player.
But the season before, he had two such penalties all season

long. That sort of history does not describe someone who is frequently letting their anger get the best of them.

The second reason I bring this up is because American football is a brutal sport with aggressive acts occurring on every play. In fact, in response to discussion about whether or not his helmet attack would result in criminal charges, attorney Tammi Gaw said: "If we're going to be very technical, every single thing that takes place on a football field is assault."[21] Certainly, Garrett's hit and Pouncey's response far exceeded the typical act of violence on the field, but there is something very interesting about watching an aggressive sport, sometimes even cheering for big hits, and then reacting with such shock and vitriol when these things go further than expected.

I would argue that there are four overlapping components here that make this case really stand out and left a lot of people in shock when they saw it. First, there was the intentionality of Garrett's act. He was unquestionably trying to hurt Rudolph when he swung at him, and as physically brutal as football often is, it does not usually include such intentionality. Second, he essentially used a weapon – the helmet – and we don't see that in football very often. Third, Rudolph was defenseless as he was not wearing a helmet, making the brutality of the act that much greater. Finally, and the part I am most interested in, Garrett's violence was motivated by anger where most of the violence on the football field is not.

It is worth contrasting the Garrett aggression with the Pouncey aggression that occurred just seconds later. Most people have not expressed much concern over Pouncey's behavior. It certainly did not garner the same sort of media frenzy as Garrett's aggression. Yet, he did punch and kick a man in the head six separate times, so why was his punishment so much less severe. It too was intentional and motivated by anger. Part of it is of course that Pouncey did not use a weapon, but I would argue that another part is that Pouncey was retaliating due to an obvious provocation and protecting a teammate, which is often considered a more acceptable form of violence.

So what does this all tell us? Three things:

1 That violence is not always or even usually related to anger.
2 That the *wrongness* of violence is largely contextual and people will employ relatively arbitrary rules to judge when violence is justified or unjustified.
3 That, more often than not, what we see as anger problems are really impulse-control problems.

The complexity of violence

In 2018, there were 1,206,836 violent crimes in the United States.[22] These include four different types of offenses: murder, rape, robbery, and aggravated assault. Essentially, these are crimes that involve force or the threat of force. If we think of these types of crimes in terms of what motivates them, it is easy to see that anger is probably not usually the cause. Robbery, for example, was about 23 per cent of those crimes and it would be very unusual for anger to be the driving force behind a robbery. Similarly, when you think about the complexity of the motivations that may lead to murder, it is easy to recognize that even when anger is relevant, there are a variety of motivators above and beyond the emotion of anger (such as financial gain or jealousy).

To make matters even more complicated, violence can be defined in a variety of ways. In the 2013 book, *Violence, Inequality, and Human Freedom,*[23] Peter Iadicola and Anson Shupe write of violence much more broadly than many people might think about it. They describe violence as not just an action that causes harm, but also as a structural arrangement (an intentionally designed set of circumstances) that causes harm. That would include the interpersonal violence captured by the FBI's crime statistics above but would also include a number of things that are not illegal (police violence, military violence). In fact, Iadicola and Shupe even describe particular types of social arrangements like vast swaths of people having inadequate healthcare as a form of structural violence.*

Thus, violence is this exceedingly complicated and broadly defined concept that is largely separate from anger, yet is sometimes still motivated by anger. For example, the vast majority (67 per cent) of those more than a million instances of violent crimes in 2018 were aggravated assault, defined as "the unlawful attack by one person upon another for the purpose of inflicting severe or aggravated bodily injury." It is almost impossible to know what percentage of those were motivated by anger, but certainly many of them were. We see examples of that all the time in the news. Physical fights breaking out at bars, instances of road rage turning violent, and other examples flood the news. Some of these seem outright insane. In 2016, for example, here in Wisconsin, a fight broke out because a Green Bay Packer fan tried to destroy a Minnesota Vikings yard display. The owner of the display, Dave Moschel, came outside to stop the vandal, Jacob Justice, and was stabbed seven times. Moschel lived, thankfully.†

Motivators of violence

Ultimately, I wish it were possible to determine how much of the world's violence problem is related to anger versus

---

* While it is well beyond the scope of this book to explore these different forms of violence, it is worth asking why swinging a football helmet at someone is considered violence but voting to take health care from millions is not violent. The latter undoubtedly ends in many deaths.

† There is an especially haunting sidenote to this story, which is that Moschel said later: "Luckily, I didn't have my concealed carry on me at the time. Ninety-nine per cent of the time I leave the house, I never leave without it. And this is the one time I did. I'm kind of glad I did, because he would be dead, and I would have had to live with that."

something else, but as you already know, people aggress for a variety of reasons and anger is not always or even the main one. In fact, we can identify quite a few reasons why human beings will sometimes become violent that are not directly related to anger.

People will undoubtedly aggress out of fear. They become scared for their safety or the safety of their loved ones, and they respond with aggression. It is a relatively natural and expected outcome when you feel under attack to want to defend yourself. In a similar vein is what people sometimes refer to as territorial aggression. People will aggress when they feel their homes or belongings are under attack in some way. When someone is mugged, has their home broken into, or has their inflatable football decoration stabbed, they might respond with aggression to protect their belongings.*

Although I have made it clear that there is no good indicator of what most often motivates violence, my best guess would be that much violence world-wide is instrumental. Instrumental violence is when the violence exists to accomplish some sort of goal. In this case, the violence is a means to an end. This explains so much of the day-to-day aggression we see: war and other forms of military violence, aggression from the police, armed robbery, and so on. In these instances, the violence exists because the perpetrator of the violence is trying to gain something. An offender may use violence as a means to steal something, and soldiers may use violence to claim or reclaim territory. In both cases, the violence exists to accomplish some other goal.

The violence most relevant to this book, though, is irritable violence, where the aggression stems from a feeling

---

*   A frustration of mine is how often people conflate protection of their belongings with protection of themselves. While I admit that sometimes both can be under attack at the same time, protecting yourself is fundamentally different from protecting your stuff.

state*... often anger. Irritable violence is what we saw from both Garrett and Pouncey. They got angry and reacted with the intent to harm. In some ways, this is a natural and expected reaction to anger. By definition, anger includes a very real desire to lash out and it requires impulse control to keep yourself from doing that. It is not just anger, though. Violence can be sparked by a number of different emotions. People lash out when they feel jealous, guilty, sad, grief, or a host of other emotions.

Of course, these different categories overlap. If we think about intimate partner violence as an example, you can see how it can be both instrumental and irritable. Certainly, the violence can stem from emotions like anger or jealousy in particular situations. A husband becomes angry with his wife for not doing what he asked, and he hits or pushes her. He becomes jealous because he sees her talking to another man at a party, and he beats her when they get home. But this violence also stems from an instrumental desire to maintain a power structure. Maybe consciously or maybe not, on some level he is using violence to keep her from doing things he does not like and to keep her from leaving him. The violence is not just a reaction to emotions, it is part of a strategy for him to maintain a particular marital structure.

Beliefs about violence

The use of violence is predicted largely, but not exclusively, by the beliefs a person has about the appropriateness of violence as a problem-solving approach. If you believe that violence is a reasonable way to deal with disagreements or to assert yourself,

---

* I want to go on record as saying that I know fear is also a feeling-state, yet I talk about it separately. I cannot really explain why, but psychiatrists and psychologists often talk about fear and anxiety separately from other feeling states. *The Diagnostic and Statistical Manual of Mental Disorders* has long had "anxiety disorders" and "mood disorders" as separate categories even though anxiety is clearly a mood state. It is weird.

you are more likely to be aggressive when provoked or simply to get what you want. In fact, your likelihood to aggress is even predicted by the types of thoughts you have. In the research I have done with the Angry Cognitions Scale, all five of those types of thoughts we discussed in chapter 4 (misattributing causation, catastrophizing, overgeneralizing, demandingness, and inflammatory labeling) were related to aggression and thoughts of revenge.[24]

In particular, demandingness and inflammatory labeling were most relevant, which makes intuitive sense. If someone uses dehumanizing language about others, it follows that they might treat them in dehumanizing ways. If someone believes their needs are more important than the needs of others, it follows that they might use violence to impose their will and have their needs met.

Of course, there are occasions when people who do not necessarily endorse violence simply snap and become aggressive. They lose their cool and do something that does not feel consistent with who they really are and what they care about. In short, they do something impulsive.

Losing control

Impulsiveness is when someone acts without thinking through the implications or the consequences of those actions. Essentially, they respond to something quickly, spontaneously, and without any sort of reflection on what their response will mean. Myles Garrett, for example, acted impulsively when he swung that helmet at Mason Rudolph. At least according to his apology, he lost his cool and did something he believed inconsistent with his character. He did not consider the consequences of that act on either himself or Rudolph. Had he thought about the potential injury or even death he might have caused Rudolph or the more than a million dollars he might lose as a result of that swing, he might not have done it. But that is what impulsivity is. It is an action whereby we fail to think through the short and long-term consequences of what we are about to do, and we are all capable of impulsive acts.

Impulsivity is not linked exclusively to anger by any means. People can act impulsively in a variety of contexts (eating, drug use, spending, gambling, sex). When people take their kids to the ice-cream shop and tell themselves, "This is just for them, I'm not getting anything" yet walk out with a sundae, that is likely them making an impulsive decision in the moment that violates their original plan. When someone walks into a store saying, "I only need one thing" but walks out with well more than that, that is impulsivity rearing its ugly head.

Impulse-control disorders

There is actually an entire category of disorders in the *Diagnostic and Statistical Manual of Mental Disorders* (*DSM-5*) dedicated to impulse-control disorders. I have already mentioned the DSM-5, but if you are not familiar with it, it is a big book of diagnosable mental-health conditions published by the American Psychiatric Association. It includes everything from major depressive disorders to schizophrenia to anorexia nervosa and more. It is organized by sections based on disorder similarity (for example, a chapter for depressive disorders, a chapter for anxiety disorders)* and there is a chapter titled "Disruptive, Impulse-Control, and Conduct Disorders."† It includes disorders "involving problems in the self-control of

---

* Interestingly, no chapter for anger disorders. This is something I will have a lot to say about later.

† It is worth noting that impulsivity is not exclusively tied to negative behaviors. Some impulsive behaviors are positive. For example, though we tend not to think of them as *impulsive,* acts of heroism often happen with little forethought or consideration of the implications. Such behaviors are often thought of us as courageous and gutsy, but ultimately they are similarly impulsive just with more positive consequences.

emotions and behaviors."[25] The authors are quick to point out that there are many disorders throughout the *DSM-5* where impulsivity is a prominent feature (such as obsessive-compulsive disorder, mania, substance abuse), but notes that the disorders in this particular section involve the violation of others' rights through aggression or the destruction of property.

The impulse-control disorders listed here include some you have likely heard of. Kleptomania, the uncontrolled impulse to steal, and pyromania, the failure to control impulses to set fires, are relatively rare but still known by most people. However, a less frequently discussed disorder is intermittent explosive disorder (IED), an impulse-control disorder that includes "recurring behavioral outbursts representing a failure to control aggressive impulses." This can include verbal aggression or physical aggression, property damage, or physical assault to animals or people. According to the *DSM-5*, this disorder is relatively rare with about 2.7 per cent of the US population meeting the diagnostic criteria.* It typically develops in adolescence, most often in people with a trauma history or a genetic predisposition, and continues in some way across the lifespan.

When I talk about there not being an anger disorder in the *DSM-5*, people often point to this disorder as an example of anger that is included. You, of course, will not make that mistake because by now you are well aware of the differences between anger and aggression. IED is an aggression disorder and not an anger disorder. While the outbursts are described

---

* I say "relatively rare" because it is compared with disorders like major depressive disorder (7 per cent) and generalized anxiety disorder (9 per cent). But at the same time, it is on par with or even more common than a number of disorders in the *DSM-5* that get a lot more attention in popular culture and the news media. Bipolar I disorder, for example, has a 0.6 per cent prevalence rate and schizophrenia has between a 0.3 and 0.7 per cent prevalence rate yet receive far more attention.

as "anger-based,"* the criteria are clearly about one type of expression of anger and fail to acknowledge the many different negative consequences that can result from poorly managed anger.

Impulsivity as a personality trait

As with any set of behaviors, there are some people who are far more likely to act impulsively than others. There is a continuum with maladaptive and problematic, maybe even diagnosable, at one end to typically cool, calm, and collected at the other end. We can think of people who often engage in impulsive behaviors (that is, behave impulsively more than most people) as having an impulsive personality.† To help decide where people fall on the continuum, there is a scale that measures such impulsive tendencies. It is called the Barratt Impulsiveness Scale (BIS-11) and it is a 30-item questionnaire that poses statements to score such as "I solve problems by trial-and-error" and "I talk fast." Higher scores mean a greater tendency to act impulsively and research has linked this questionnaire to a variety of mental-health and behavioral problems.

Dr. Eric Dahlen and I did a few studies on impulsivity and anger where we used this same questionnaire. In our first study we wanted to know what the relationship was between impulsivity and the aggressive expression of anger. We gave

---

* For an article I recently wrote, I searched the *DSM-5* for every instance of the word anger. It is used only a handful of times. You know what word is used over and over again, though? "Danger" (as in a *danger* to self or others). I know this because, as the cliché will tell you, "*anger* is one letter short of *danger*" and, consequently, my *DSM-5* PDF search revealed each and every instance of a word I was not looking for.

† You can learn more about impulsivity through the International Society for Research on Impulsivity, an organization with more than 30 members. You can also attend one of their meetings which, much to my disappointment, are scheduled well in advance. I was hoping to click on the "meetings" tab and have it say "just be ready for us."

people a bunch of questionnaires on concepts like impulsivity, boredom proneness, anger, and aggression to determine which of those things predicted aggression best. We found that impulsivity was linked to anger, the outward expression of anger (yelling and screaming), and aggression.[26] When you looked more closely, though, what really stood out was how impulsivity was related to the outward expression of anger and negatively correlated with anger control. In other words, people who had a hard time controlling their impulses had a really hard time controlling their anger. Sometimes they were violent, but even when they were not violent, they would yell and scream.

The second study we did was pretty similar to this one, but we were more interested in aggressive driving (road rage) this time.[27] Shockingly, at the time, no one had really looked at impulsiveness as it related to aggressive and angry driving.* Again, we gave people surveys of impulsiveness and boredom proneness (same ones as above), but this time we also asked them about their driving behaviors. How often did they engage in dangerous behaviors (such as losing concentration, driving without a seatbelt) on the road and how often had they suffered negative consequences for those dangerous behaviors (such as speeding tickets, accidents)?

Impulsiveness was related to every possible angry and aggressive driving variable. Every single one: verbally aggressive driving, physically aggressive driving, use of the vehicle to express anger, and more. Basically, if you are an impulsive person, you are more likely to yell at people, give them the finger, cut them off, try and chase them down, and even get out of the car to try and fight with them. In fact, when we looked at risky driving overall, impulsiveness explained about

---

* A lot of people think of aggressive driving and angry driving as the same thing, but (not surprisingly) they are separate. You can get angry behind the wheel and intentionally cut someone off or yell at them (aggressive) or you can get angry and engage in risky, but not aggressive acts like speeding, changing lanes sporadically, and ignoring stop lights.

23 per cent, and when you looked at the tendency to use the vehicle as a weapon by cutting people off or intentionally slowing down to aggravate people, it explained just under 20 per cent. Quite simply, impulsiveness explains a lot of the violence we see on the road.

The weapons effect

Most of what I have discussed so far has been about individual differences in impulsivity. But the environment matters too. For that, I want to turn to a conversation I had with Dr. Brad Bushman, a social psychologist in the School of Communication at The Ohio State University. Dr. Bushman is an extraordinary scholar in the area of aggression and violence, even having served as a member of President Obama's committee on gun violence. I have had the pleasure of interviewing him twice on topics related to aggressive driving and the catharsis myth (a concept we'll cover in chapter 12). Both times, what I appreciated most about him is what an amazing scientific mind he has. He does something I wish we saw more of from people. He answers questions with data and tells stories with research findings. When I asked him questions, he would answer them with a narrative that included the research findings from past scholars, how they informed his research, and his own findings. When I asked him questions where he did not know the research or the research had not yet been done, he would tell me that he could not answer that question with research, but would still make a prediction based on similar findings he was aware of.

He has access to this incredible driving simulator where he and his research team study aggressive driving. He described it to me as a real car "that is completely surrounded by screens." In fact, even the rear view and side view mirrors are functional with LED displays that help make the simulation as real as possible. He can use the simulator to create very real feeling situations for participants to see how they would respond in a similar situation on the road. It is a way to safely study the potential dangers of aggressive driving.

He described a research project they did using the simulator in 2017 to explore the weapons effect. This study was based on a famous 1967 study conducted by Dr. Leonard Berkowitz and Anthony LePage called "Weapons as Aggression-Eliciting Stimuli." They brought male college students into a lab for a study on "the psychological reactions to stress." The participants were paired up with another participant and were each, individually, given a task to complete (they were asked to generate a list of ideas an agent could use to improve a singer's record sales). They worked for five minutes, their responses were collected, and they were brought to separate rooms.

Not surprisingly, if you are familiar with a lot of famous psychological research of that era, the study was not actually about the psychological reaction to stress and their partner was not actually another participant. Their partner was actually a member of the research team (what psychological researchers often refer to as a "confederate" or an "accomplice") and the study was about the effect of having a weapon in sight on one's likelihood of acting violently. After being brought to separate rooms, the actual participant had shock electrodes* placed on their arms. The accomplice, meanwhile, went and sat at a machine that delivered actual shocks to the participant. The accomplice then provided "feedback" to the participants on their earlier work by way of electric shocks. When they were done, they switched places. The accomplice was hooked up to the electrodes and the participant gave them feedback on their work via shocks.

---

* This study should not be confused with the series of studies conducted by Stanley Milgram in the 1960s that found that approximately two-thirds of people will administer a potentially fatal shock to another person if ordered to do so. In those studies, the shocks were fake. This time they are real. As it turns out, psychological scientists have a long history of either pretending to shock people … or actually shocking people.

There were actually six different categories (seven if you count a control group that did nothing) here based on (a) how many shocks the participants received and (b) what was sitting on the table in the room they were in. The number-of-shocks condition is relatively simple to understand. Participants were either provoked by the accomplice with seven electric shocks or were unprovoked with just one shock. The other condition is a little more complicated but as the participants entered the room, there were three scenarios: nothing on the table, some sporting equipment, or a 12-gauge shotgun and a .38-caliber revolver. When there was something on the table, the researchers said, "Oh I can't believe the other experimenter didn't clean up after himself. Please just ignore what's on the table."

So the groups end up looking like this:

	Nothing	Sports equipment	Guns
Low anger (one shock)			
High anger (seven shocks)			

Berkowitz and LePage wanted to see how many electric shocks the participants would provide as feedback to their partner and whether or not it would differ based on what group they were in. What they found was that there was no difference when there was nothing on the table and when there was sports equipment on the table, but when there was a shotgun or a handgun on the table, participants administered more shocks. This was especially true when they were provoked with seven shocks. Berkowitz and LePage state in the article that "many hostile acts which supposedly stem from unconscious motivation really arise because of the operation of aggressive cues."[28]

According to Dr. Bushman "this study has been replicated many times both inside and outside the laboratory." In fact, in our discussions he pointed to a more recent study as motivation for his own research on the weapons effect:

I read about a study,* actually a nationally represented sample of 2,770 American drivers. The researchers reported that those drivers who had a gun in their vehicle at least once in the past year were significantly more aggressive drivers than those who had no gun in the vehicle. For example, they were more likely to make obscene gestures at other drivers, 23 per cent versus 16 per cent. They were more likely to tailgate, 14 per cent versus 8 per cent. And the researchers controlled for many different factors like gender and age, but also driving frequency, and whether they lived in a city or urban environment or things like that.

Dr. Bushman and his research team thought:

Well it's hard to make causal inferences based on this survey study,† so we basically did a replication of the Berkowitz and LePage experiment in our driving-simulation lab. Participants got in the car and by the flip of a coin they got either a tennis racquet or a 9mm handgun (unloaded) on the seat. And the experimenter said exactly the same thing: "Oh I can't believe the other experimenter didn't clean up after himself, just ignore that." What we found was those participants who had a gun on the passenger seat were much more aggressive drivers in the frustration simulation scenario than were participants who had a tennis racket on the seat. And we

* The study he's referring to is by Hemenway and colleagues (2006) and it is an extraordinarily thorough review of aggression on the road.

† As I said, he has a scientific mind that does not take anything for granted. He saw interesting findings, recognized the limitations, and took it to the next step to address those limitations.

can make causal inferences because we flipped a coin to determine whether there was a tennis racket or a real gun on the seat.

I asked him to describe the aggressive and risky behaviors and he detailed some typical behaviors we might see on the road: tailgating, speeding, crossing into oncoming traffic to pass, or driving onto the shoulder to pass. They honked the horn, were verbally aggressive, or used aggressive hand gestures like giving another driver the finger. Though, the scariest response was that "one person actually grabbed the gun and tried to shoot the other driver."

ACTIVITY: MANAGING IMPULSIVITY

For this activity, I want you to think about a time that you acted impulsively in response to your anger. Whether that behavior was aggressive or not, think of a time when your anger led to you doing something without thinking through the consequences.

1   Diagram the incident. What was the precipitant, the pre-anger state, and the appraisal process?
2   What was the impulsive thing you did in response to this anger and what was the outcome?
3   Looking back on it, what do you wish you would have done differently in response to this anger?
4   While we will talk more about *catching yourself* in these bouts of anger later, what do you think you could have done in the moment to stop yourself from acting impulsively?

Unchecked anger in personal relationships

Impulsive anger leading to violence like this can happen anywhere: on the road among strangers, on the field or court during a sporting event, and at work between colleagues. But what happens when violence occurs in relationships? What is the impact of such expressions of anger in families, between spouses, or toward children? What about other forms of anger? What can anger do to personal relationships if left unchecked?

CHAPTER 7

DAMAGED RELATIONSHIPS

A social emotion

Anger is sometimes referred to as a "social emotion" because it is so frequently experienced in social situations. In fact, researchers have found between 80 and 90 per cent of angry incidents are the result of social situations.[29] People rarely feel anger when they are on their own and not interacting with people, and I bet if I were to ask you to list the last five times you became angry, you would find that almost all of them involved another person. This is different from some other basic emotions like sadness, fear, or joy, which often occur without the presence of another person. What this means, of course, is that because anger occurs in the context of social situations, poorly managed anger is likely to result in damaged relationships.

A client of mine once sat in my office reflecting on his troubled relationship with his girlfriend. He had a habit of losing his temper with her, never harming her physically but yelling at her often. "I don't want to be a tyrant" he said, his voice cracking as he started to tear up. His father had been a tyrant, so he knew what it felt like to be yelled at. He hated this about himself and was coming to therapy to learn to better manage his anger. It is relatively common for people to suffer emotionally like this as a result of their anger, but right now I am more interested in the impact his anger was having on their relationship.

When Eric Dahlen and I refined the Anger Consequences Questionnaire, one of the things we found was that damaged friendships was a fairly common consequence according to most participants. On the scale, it is measured with just three items: damage a friendship, make my friends afraid of me, and make my friends mad at me. Participants indicated how often they have experienced that consequence in the past month as a result of their anger (from "never" to "four or more times"). On average, participants said they had experienced this sort of relationship problem just over one time in the past month.

Years later, my research team and I collected data via an online survey of participants who frequently vented online.[30] To be clear, this is in no way a representative sample. These participants were people who would visit rant-sites, websites designed to allow anonymous ranting, to write anonymous posts with titles like "I f#%king hate my mom" and "the line at Starbucks sucks."* It is fair to assume they were angrier than the typical person.† While we did not use the full Anger Consequences Questionnaire this time, we did ask some specific questions about how often in the month prior to taking the survey they got into physical fights and verbal fights (average of 1.26 and 1.45 times, respectively), how often they

---

* The most visited of these sites was www.justrage.com, which at the time of this research had more than 5,000 rants posted that had been read by more than ten million people. I tried to visit it as I was writing this and found that it seems to have been taken down. Probably not due to complaints, however, as when I once went to the page titled "Do you have a problem with justrage?" there was no contact information ... just a giant middle finger directed at the reader.

† Plus, our study confirmed that they were angrier than the average person, so we do not need to assume. They scored significantly higher than the average for the Trait Anger Scale, a measure of one's propensity to become angry. They also expressed it in more negative ways, according to the Anger Expression Scale.

abused a substance because of their anger (1.39 times), and how often they damaged a relationship (1.26 times).

Those are rather striking numbers. To say that you damaged at least one relationship as a result of your anger in the past month is a significant consequence of anger. While it is possible this past month was atypical for these participants (maybe that is why they were venting online, because they had been particularly angry), it is also quite possible that this past month was not atypical at all. This might just be what happens in a typical month for them. What is worse, though, is that I suspect this is on the low end as far as estimates go. For reasons I will discuss later in this chapter, I suspect the toll poorly managed anger takes on relationships is considerably higher than found in these studies and is greater than most people realize.

An "especially bad" fight

Nikki* is a former student of mine who graduated a few years ago. I was looking for someone who had been in a physical fight as a result of their anger, and she responded to a general call I put out on social media. We set up a time to talk via phone. I had known Nikki fairly well as a student. She had taken a couple of courses from me, and we stayed in touch via Facebook after she graduated. I had a sense of her as a strong person and a hard-working student. But as I often find, my students sometimes have exceedingly complicated lives outside of school, and this was certainly one of those times.

During her senior year of college, Nikki was dating a man she met through a dating app. As she described it, "He had kind of moved in." She said, "We didn't really discuss it ever, but he had gradually moved into my apartment." From the

---

* Nikki is not her real name. She told me she had no problem with me using her real name, but I wanted to be extra careful considering the violent nature of the story she told me. She went with "Nikki" because she was just about to see Mötley Crüe in concert.

discussion she and I had about him, it sounded as though this sort of behavior was typical from him. He found a variety of ways to manipulatively leech off her by using her things, especially her car, having her pay for things, and even taking over her space. They had dated for a year and, during that time, he was getting increasingly aggressive with her both verbally and physically.* She told me that they had had a handful of physical altercations throughout that year.

"To what degree are these fights self-defense on your part versus you initiating things?" I asked. I wanted to know if this was a case of intimate partner violence where she was the victim or if this was a case where they were both starting fights at times. The latter is relatively rare, but it does happen. I asked: "How often are these physical altercations really you defending yourself from someone who is attacking you?"

She said it was about 80/20 with her defending herself most of the time. She said she started it about 20 per cent of the time. "It was a weird time because he was doing other domestically abusive things. He was emotionally and psychologically manipulative." She was a student at the time and was trying to keep up with her schoolwork and her job. They would argue a lot, most of the time about him using her belongings. He would take the car without asking her for hours or even days. She had to walk to school sometimes. "Just a flat-out toxic relationship," she said. That 20 per cent of the time that she reported initiating the physical fights was when he did something, usually using her stuff without asking, and she would lash out at him physically.

The last fight they had, though, was – to use her words – "especially bad." It started with a verbal fight but escalated quickly. He had taken her car again without permission. It was a weekend; he had been over the night before, and they

---

* Keep in mind that Nikki was a psychology major, so some of her answers (such as "aggressive both verbally and physically") sound quite *clinical* (at least they do to me, her proud psychology professor).

had been drinking. When she woke up, he had left and taken her car. She called and texted him, but he had not responded. She said she was anxious about having to go into work, as she sometimes got called in unexpectedly. She kept messaging him over the course of the day, the messages getting increasingly "hostile" as the day went on.

It was just before midnight when he came back. He had not responded to any of her messages. He said he had been at work, which was just a few blocks away, but the gas tank was empty even though it had been full the night before. "He had obviously been driving all day," she told me, and when she called him on it, it turned into a fight.

"Why aren't you answering? Why do you think this is okay?" she screamed. She was livid and seeing red. "I hate you!"

He started to berate her verbally, calling her "every cussword in the book." He said she should trust him, and that he was pitching in now, so she should cut him some slack. Now, they were screaming at each other, and she got nervous that the police would be called on them. It had happened twice before that neighbors had called the police because of the noise. She told me she was out of control, though, and "couldn't stop screaming at him."

"Fuck you," he yelled at her, "I'm leaving."

She ran after him and tried pushing him, trying to keep him from getting back in her car. He grabbed her hair and pushed her away. "It was so dramatic," she told me, "like a movie. And you don't think it's going to happen to you or that you'll go through it, but then you are in it." She told me she was so angry and so frustrated that she didn't know what to do, so she just kept screaming at him and started hitting him.

He was physically stronger than her and was able to get back in the car despite her efforts to keep him away. She got into the passenger seat, though, and they continued to yell at each other. "No," she yelled, "you need to get out of my car! This is my car. You need to stop taking my car without my permission!" He started driving and she kept yelling, "Stop the car! This is my car! You need to get out!"

He grabbed a handful of her hair, pulled her toward him, and said, "You're all for equal rights. You're a feminist. This is what equal rights gets you," and he hit her in the face multiple times. This was all happening while he was driving. They were getting on the highway and Nikki was scared. She stopped fighting back and somehow convinced him to go back to her apartment. She was in tears, and they were swearing at each other as they got out of the car and went back to her apartment.

When they got inside, she punched him again. "You're a piece of shit," she said. "You shouldn't be here. This is my house. These are my things." He hit her back and this progressed to the point they were full-on fighting again, both hitting each other and pulling each other's hair. At one point, though, he got on top of her and started to choke her. She could not breathe and thought she was going to pass out.

She thought maybe it somehow hit him how serious this was because he stopped choking her and got off her, leaving her alone. She ran to the bathroom and locked herself in. She heard him leave. She looked in the mirror and saw her face. Her eyes were swollen like they were going to turn black. She was missing clumps of hair, and she already had bruises forming all over her. She said he came back hours later and was in similarly bad shape. He had bruises and might have had a broken eye socket.

It was this incident that was the last straw for her. She realized how dangerous this could be, so she blocked him on her phone and social media, changed apartments, and cut him out of her life completely.

When Nikki thought back on this incident, and the relationship more generally, she had a lot of complicated feelings about it. "We were both so angry at each other all the time. We didn't talk things out. We exploded at each other with anger." She had been asked many times why she did not leave him,* and her answer is relatively common for people in violent relationships. For much of their relationship, he had manipulated her into cutting off ties with people she cared about, so he was the only close person in her life. She felt trapped. She could not go to her landlord because her boyfriend was not supposed to be living there anyway. She did not want to try and press charges because there had been times when she had started things and she did not trust the system.

"We had no control"

If I am being honest, the story I heard from Nikki was not the story I was originally looking for when I put out the call. I was curious about people who got angry and got into physical fights as a result of that anger. What she told me, though, was more a story of intimate partner violence where even though she may have "started it" some of the time,† the vast majority of the time she was the victim of violence, manipulation, and gas-lighting.

All that said, what was evident from talking with her, though, was that she was very quick to respond with aggression when angered, and that this was not limited to her fights with him. "I've been uncontrollably angry before to the point that I was not using my words," she said. "I would freak out and hit the person." She described, for example, very intense physical fights with her siblings. They would punch each other often, sometimes even in the face. She said to me: "All three of us have had issues with anger and lashing out at each other, and I don't think it was very typical

---

* I have such mixed feelings about this question. It is inherently victim-blaming, as though survivors of abuse somehow own the responsibility of not being abused. At the same time, we need to know the answer to this question so we can help people get out of violent relationships like this one.

† It really depends on how you define "started it" as the examples she gave were consistently him treating her horribly and her exploding in response.

considering it did get physical sometimes like where we would punch each other in the face, and we would physically really rail on each other."

This made me curious. I am the youngest with three siblings: a sister and two brothers. We picked on each other sometimes, and my older brothers in particular would hit me, often on the arm or shoulder, on occasion, but I do not think it was usually out of anger. In my experience, no one was trying to hurt or injure anyone, and I do not believe any of us ever punched one of us in the face. In fact, I can only remember a handful of times we physically fought in response to an argument or out of anger.

My family experience notwithstanding, I was able to find a research article from 2015 on sibling aggression to get a better sense for frequency. According to Drs. Neil Tippett and Dieter Wolke[31] from the University of Warwick, who surveyed nearly 5,000 10-to-15-year-olds on their experience with sibling aggression as perpetrators and/or victims, approximately 50 per cent of their respondents had been the victim of physical aggression from a sibling. It was more common in 10-to-12-year-olds (58.1 per cent) than in 13-to-15-year-olds (41.9 per cent) and it was highly related to being the perpetrator of sibling aggression. In other words, the kids that hit their siblings had been hit by a sibling. What this study did not tell me, though, that I was really curious about in the context of Nikki, was the severity of those aggressive acts. While both can be bad, a punch on the shoulder is not the same as a punch in the face, and I still do not have a sense for how common the latter is.

What Nikki described did not feel typical to me. She has two younger siblings and she said that there was a lot of physical fighting among them when they were younger, but she said it continued into early adulthood. She described a couple of Christmases when there had been physical fights. Here is what she said about it:

One of them would throw a punch in the arm, and I would throw a punch back in the arm, and then it would, you know, escalate to now we're punching each other in the face and pulling each other's hair. And it would always be fine the next morning, but all of it came out of anger the night before. We would apologize and be like, "That escalated super quickly." We had no control, we realized that we had no control, we would move on, but … it would get to the point where it was so explosive, where just … you know … "I need to hurt you."

She told me that her parents would argue sometimes, but it never got physical. They would complain about each other, but that was about it. Her dad would often need to leave the room to calm down, which was probably best because he did have a history of aggression, and this is likely where Nikki learned some of her anger expression styles.* "My dad always had a temper, so he told us. He'd say, 'When I was your age, I would always get into fist fights and bar brawls.'" He actually told her a story about a fight he got into where he thought he killed someone because it got so violent. It was a bar fight that had to be broken up by friends. He had been in and out of jail for bar fights and other things, but this particular fight was the turning point where he realized he needed to change his ways.

When she was growing up, though, he sent very clear messages to her about the need to solve some problems with aggression. Kids always learn emotion expression from their caregivers through modeling. If a parent or other primary caregiver's main anger expression style is to yell, the child will learn to yell. If they cry, the child learns to cry, and if they fight, the child learns to fight. But in this case, Nikki's dad was even more direct, even teaching the kids how to physically

---

* This is consistent with the Tippett and Wolke article above, which found that "parenting characteristics were most strongly linked with sibling aggression."

defend themselves and how to punch. She said that he told her: "If somebody steps on you, you better defend yourself."

Invisible disruptions

As you already know, I have my own experiences with an angry father. The situation with my dad was quite different, though. He was not a fighter. In fact, to my knowledge, my dad was never in a physical fight as an adult, and I suspect it was not a regular occurrence when he was a kid either. My dad was a yeller, and that brought with it a very different set of relationship consequences.

Before I had children, I had a dog; a sweet little beagle named Kinsey.* One day I was watching a football game and she was next to me, curled up on her bed. I got angry over what I thought was a bad call and yelled something at my TV. I was quite loud and I think I went on for a little while. When it was all over and I had calmed down, I looked down at her and saw that she was scared. She was shaking and eyeing me uncomfortably. She was not just scared; she was scared of me. It was an unexpectedly painful moment for me because I realized I had scared her terribly, which I did not like, but also because – and I realize this might sound silly – it took me back to when I was a kid I would hear my dad yelling at someone. It would scare me terribly, and I spent a lot of my childhood frightened of him.

It is worth noting that he almost never yelled at me. I can only think of a few times when that happened. I was rarely the target of his anger but being around him when he was angry at others still took a toll on our relationship because I was so scared of him. There are two important lessons to be learned here:

---

* Because I am a psychologist, people assume we named her after Dr. Alfred Kinsey, the famous sex researcher from the 1940s and 50s. We did not, though. She was named after Kinsey Millhone of Sue Grafton's alphabet mystery series, only we called her "Kinsey Mill-hound."

1 He probably had no idea how scared I was of him.
2 None of this would be captured by those surveys above.

Regarding the first point, how could he know? I never told him. After all, I was scared of him so trying to have a personal conversation about my feelings with him was out of the question for me. And when I got older, I was not so much scared of him, I was just uncomfortable around him. The years of being scared as a kid meant that as an adult, I never felt like I could be myself. Every time I was around him, it felt like I was on a job interview. I felt like I had to be on my best behavior for fear of making him mad. What is funny and sad about that is that the things I was scared of rarely happened when I was an adult. He actually started to mellow out as he got older, and I saw fewer and fewer of those angry outbursts from him. But my discomfort never went away.

This is another way anger can damage relationships. People who get angry often and intensely, especially if they express that anger outwardly, make the people around them uncomfortable or scared. The people around them spend their days waiting for the other shoe to drop, trying not to do anything that will cause an outburst. When the outburst does come, whether they are responsible for it or not, they often feel compelled to try and fix it. As the client above told me, it is like living with a *tyrant*.

Meanwhile, the angry person probably has little idea how their outbursts might be affecting the people around them. They likely do not see that fear or discomfort. As surveys like the Anger Consequences Questionnaire ask questions about how often people have experienced particular consequences, if the person taking the survey is not aware, the survey cannot capture the full extent of the consequences. Chances are the results of those studies earlier are a significant underestimate.

Online offensiveness and aggression

Another thing to keep in mind is that the Anger Consequences Questionnaire was written in 1996 and revised in 2006, well before the omnipresence of social media – and the very real anger consequences that come with social media. A few years ago, I showed my research assistants the questionnaire and they pointed out that it was missing an entire category of consequences; specifically, those things that can happen when you post out of anger. We set to work on an Online Anger Consequences Questionnaire that could be used as a supplement to the other scale.*

To write it, we started generating a list of the negative things that had happened to people and others they knew as a result of expressing their anger online. We outsourced this item generation to – you guessed it – social media, to generate as many examples as possible. I am glad we did too, because people came up with things I never would have thought of. I had known, of course, that people sometimes got in trouble at work over something they posted or sometimes sent emails they later regretted. I did not know, though, that people would sometimes intentionally post unflattering pictures of people as a means of getting revenge. I also did not know how often people would post something online with the hopes that a person they were mad at would see it (a form of passive-aggressive posting or antisocial media).

The final scale included two primary types of online consequences: offending others and aggressing toward others. The former category describes those times when someone posted something out of anger and offended someone they cared about. More often than not, they reported regretting what they posted. It included examples like "I lost a friend or damaged a relationship because of

---

* The scale itself is currently unpublished, but we wrote the questions and collected data exploring the relationships between these items and other anger consequences.

something I posted online when I was angry" or "I got in trouble at work because I angrily posted about my job." The latter category, aggressing toward others, includes the more intentional desire to hurt people through online behavior. Items here included "Tell confidential/private information about someone through a social networking site" or "I called someone an obscene name online."

The frequency with which people harmed relationships was again quite startling. These were not unusually angry participants (indeed their scores on other measures of anger were in the normal range) and they reported offending someone online just over one time in the past month and also tried intentionally to hurt someone online about 1.1 times in the past month. These two subscales were related to a number of other anger-related problems like other anger consequences and maladaptive expressions. Basically, if you experienced anger often or in high intensity, and you expressed it outwardly, you also tended to damage relationships because of your anger via social media.

ACTIVITY: EXPLORING RELATIONSHIP CONSEQUENCES

This activity is to get you thinking broadly about the potential relationship consequences of your anger, in two steps:

1   Identify five important people in your life (such as family, friends, coworkers).
2   Think about how they have experienced your anger and how it likely made them feel. For example, have you yelled at them, to which they may have felt scared or hurt? Have you been passively aggressive with them, to which they may have felt angry? Have you hurt their feelings with something you posted online?

"A whole jumble of emotions"

Thinking back to Nikki's story, a few things really stand out. First is that this incident was life changing. "I learned from that," she said. "I'm trying to do better when I feel explosive. I walk away. I haven't gotten into a fist or physical fight since 2016."

"What do you do to stop yourself when you're feeling that uncontrollable rage," I asked.

"Lately," she said, "just flat-out walking away. I need to stop talking to the person and get out of the situation. Even walking away to a different room or to my car so I can sit and chill out a little bit."

The other thing that stood out was how powerless she felt, not just during that final fight, but most days with him. She said the following:

> I majored in psychology and human development with a minor in women's and gender studies. It really made me focus on gender equality across the board. It made me feel empowered across the board and made me identify as a feminist. I would tell him about this, and his backlash was that he could hit me.* His answer to me feeling powerful was to make me feel powerless. He would diminish me and put me down. It got to a point that he manipulated me into feeling like no one cared about me.

There is a lot to unpack there. His cruelty is obvious, but so is his fear. This is how people who feel threatened behave. He was so scared of her empowerment that he felt compelled to

---

* I believe his logic here was something along the lines of "If you believe in equal rights, it is okay for me to hit you as that is how I would treat a man." I have seen this rationale before when I troll online forums for various patriarchal groups (for research purposes, you cannot research online anger without reading the opinions of white supremacists and sexists). If your first response to the idea of equality is "Good, I get to beat you up now," there is a lot of humanity missing from your worldview.

push her back down. After all, if she feels too empowered, she will kick him out.

The other piece here that I want to unpack, though, is her feelings of powerlessness and anger. Here was this person treating her horribly unfairly and interfering in her life (blocking her goals). She was mad, and she had every right to be mad, but she was not sure of the best way to deal with that anger. She felt powerless, scared, and "a whole jumble of emotions." She felt anger at herself too, saying "I should have known better. I could have left. I could have done something. I feel a lot of mixed emotions."

That jumble of emotions – the anger at him, the anger at herself, the fear, the sadness – it is all very common. Anger does not happen in a vacuum. We feel it at the same time we feel other things like sadness, guilt, jealousy, fear, and even joy. In fact, one of the more common consequences of maladaptive anger is the toll it takes on the angry person themselves, both emotionally and physically. Chronically angry people suffer immensely because of their anger, and the way they suffer depends quite a lot on how they tend to express their rage.

CHAPTER 8
PHYSICAL AND MENTAL HEALTH

"Doers, capable of accomplishing their particular functions"

In the mid-1950s, two physicians noticed something peculiar about their patients with coronary heart disease. The doctors, Meyer Friedman and Ray Rosenman, were both cardiologists who shared a private practice in San Francisco. They recognized that their younger patients (anyone under 60) with cardiovascular problems almost always exhibited a particular set of personality traits. They were driven, ambitious, uptight, competitive, and easily frustrated. This observation got them wondering about something that seems relatively obvious now, but at the time was somewhat unconventional: could there be a link between these personality traits and heart disease?

As good scientists do, they tested their hypothesis and wrote up the results for a 1959 *Journal of the American Medical Association* article titled "Association of Specific Overt Behavior Pattern with Blood and Cardiovascular Findings."* In this

---

* It is worth noting that they call this a "behavior pattern" instead of a personality trait. In the 1950s, behaviorism dominated the field of psychology to the point that people did not talk about personalities. Psychologists, or in this case physicians, needed something observable to talk about so they talked about "patterns of behavior" which can be seen and measured instead of personalities which cannot.

study, they compared two groups of participants that were formed based on these behavior patterns. Group A was defined as follows:

1 An intense, sustained drive to achieve self-selected but usually poorly defined goals.
2 Profound inclination and eagerness to compete.
3 Persistent desire for recognition and advancement.
4 Continuous involvement in multiple and diverse functions constantly subject to time restrictions (deadlines).
5 Habitual propensity to accelerate the rate of execution of many physical and mental functions.
6 Extraordinary mental and physical alertness.*

Group B was the opposite of this. These participants had the "relative absence of drive, ambition, sense of urgency, desire to compete, or involvement in deadlines." There was a third group, group C, that consisted of 46 unemployed blind men. They were selected because, while they did not exhibit the characteristics of group A, they were under extraordinary stress because of their impairment. This was Friedman and Rosenman's attempt at teasing out the impact of stressors brought on by the environment/life situation.

Participants from all three groups were interviewed, observed, and surveyed on everything from the existence of these characteristics to their family history to how they sat during the interview. They were "bled once at 9:00–11:00am" and assessed via a number of other cardiovascular tests. It is here in the article where Friedman and Rosenman describe group A as "doers, capable of accomplishing their particular functions."† What they found was that group A was a much less healthy group. They ate worse, slept less, drank more,

---

* Oh good lord, it's me. They are studying me.

† Which made my wife laugh. "Is that how we used to define ambition?" she asked, "Just doing the things you are supposed to do?"

and smoked more. They had higher cholesterol, their blood clotted more slowly, and were most likely to have clinical coronary disease.

Ultimately, this study and these findings provide the origin of an enduring concept in psychology and medicine – because "group A" went on to be known as "Type A."

Impatience

Type A people tend to be ambitious, rigid and structured, outgoing, anxious, impatient, and hostile. One of the most salient emotional characteristics of Type A personality, though, is that such people are easily angered. One of the consequences of having high expectations and lofty goals is that those goals can be blocked – sometimes quite easily. People who are Type A do not just have lofty expectations for themselves, they have lofty expectations for those around them too. They want their coworkers, friends, spouses, kids, and others to do what they "are supposed to do" and, when that does not happen, they get angry.

Take my former client, Rob,* as an example. Rob was exceedingly goal oriented in both his personal and professional life. He started each day with lengthy set of to-dos, and he went to bed disappointed if he did not accomplish all of them. If it was his fault he did not accomplish them, he felt sad and guilty. But when he thought it was the fault of his coworkers he did not accomplish his goals, he got angry. Sometimes, really angry. He was not one to yell and scream, but he would go home and vent to his wife about all the ways they screwed up. He would get angry when people did not respond quickly enough to email or when they missed even minor deadlines. It all started piling up to the point that even small things began to get to him. People not staying on task during meetings or walking too slowly in the hallway started to feel like much

* Not his real name.

bigger obstacles than they actually were. He would spend the day obsessing over why other people were "so bad at their jobs" and how they were the reason "he never got anything done."

Rob was as Type A as people come, and over time it was starting to take its toll on him. He was spending much of his day frustrated and his health, both mental and physical, was suffering. Such is the experience of chronically angry people. One of the most significant consequences is their physical health. Interestingly, it is difficult to find research that explores the health consequences of anger alone. Typically, it gets tied up in research on other related concepts (like Type A personality or neuroticism more generally).

For example, a 2006 analysis[32] by Dr. Timothy Smith at the University of Utah looked at how personality was related to physical health. Strictly speaking, a personality is quite different from an emotion. Personality is a relatively stable set of qualities or characteristics like outgoingness, obsessiveness, or openness to new experiences. That said, a person can have an angry personality in the sense that they respond with anger easily and often. In this case, it is not that they are angry all the time (just as an outgoing person might not be outgoing *all* the time), but they tend to get mad more easily when they feel provoked. Rob had an angry personality. Smith's article was a review of past research on the topic, and he points to the consistent finding that "hostility soon emerged as the most unhealthy Type A characteristic." In fact, when you tease out the different aspects of Type A personality and you look at competitiveness, ambition, and hostility separately, you often find that competitiveness and ambition have minor, if any, health consequences, while hostility and anger have significant ones.

Long-term consequences of gripe sessions

One fascinating and thorough study of this came out in 2002[33] when Dr. Patricia Chang and her colleagues wanted to better understand the relationship between anger and later developing cardiovascular disease. However, one of the challenges that comes from doing such research is that if you wait until people develop cardiovascular disease and then try and look back at their life to see how angry they were, you are going to have data that has been skewed by their memory. It will be filtered through the lens of their current state and may not reflect their true history. To best capture the actual cardiovascular consequences of a lifetime of chronic anger, you want to start collecting data when the participants are young, before there have been any health consequences, and then wait to see what problems emerge later on.

That brings us to "The Johns Hopkins Precursors Study," a 70-year longitudinal study of health outcomes run out of the School of Medicine at Johns Hopkins. The study, started by Dr. Caroline Bedell Thomas, began in 1948 and continues to this day with yearly assessments of participants. According to a recent article in *HUB*, the Johns Hopkins magazine, "not knowing which metrics would prove important, Thomas measured just about everything she could think of, including cholesterol levels, alcohol intake, and blood pressure. She even made participants plunge their hands into ice water, and smoke cigarettes, to measure their physiological reactions."[34] Consequently, there are approximately 2,500 variables for each participant, including a few that are related to anger and hostility. The study has spawned more than 150 published research papers so far.

One of those research papers is the 2002 study that Chang and her colleagues did to better understand "Anger in Young Men and Subsequent Premature Cardiovascular Disease." They looked at the responses from more than a thousand participants to determine if an angry response to stress would predict later cardiovascular disease. Participants who completed the initial survey (1,337 students graduating between 1948 and 1964) indicated how they usually react to stress. There were three options related to anger: expressed or concealed anger, gripe sessions, and irritability. Each is pretty much exactly as it sounds. If you react to stress by getting angry, becoming irritable, or having a gripe session with a friend or coworker, you checked that box. The researchers then looked to see if the people who checked those boxes later developed premature cardiovascular disease (cardiovascular disease prior to the age of 55). What they found was that the more anger items endorsed, the more likely they were to have early cardiovascular problems. They also looked to see if this stayed true even when you controlled for emotions like depression and anxiety.* Indeed, even when they controlled for depression and anxiety, severe cases of anger were associated with early heart disease.

What is always difficult to pull apart in these findings, though, is *why* this is true. What is it about anger and hostility that lead to these negative health outcomes? There are a couple of different possibilities. First, chronic anger may lead to direct physiological health consequences. As we talked about in chapter 3, when you get angry, your sympathetic nervous system kicks in. Your heart rate increases, your muscles tense up, and so on. To remain in this state for long periods of time, which is what happens when you are chronically angry, brings about health consequences like coronary heart disease, chronic muscle pain, tension headaches, and other sorts of stress-related health problems. The second possibility is that there could be indirect health consequences. Chronically angry people tend to use alcohol, nicotine, or other drugs more often than others. They may overeat or engage in other negative health behaviors that are associated with negative health consequences. Ultimately, it is likely a combination of both of these possibilities that explains why we so consistently find relationships between anger and physiological health problems.

---

* Their measure of anger was related to their measures of depression and anxiety, which is a consistent finding across studies. As we are about to discuss, anger does not just have physiological consequences; it has mental-health consequences too.

General adaptation syndrome

Dr. Hans Selye, a physician who studied stress, described a general adaptation syndrome with three stages (alarm, resistance, and exhaustion) that explains why our physical health suffers in response to stress.[35] It is again worth noting that stress is different from anger but emotions like anger, fear, and sadness are common elements of stress so it is still relevant. When we face a stressor or an angering event, we first respond with alarm and our fight-or-flight system engages. This is a relatively brief stage before the second stage of general adaptation syndrome, resistance, begins. In the resistance stage our body is releasing a number of hormones, including cortisol, to help us stay energized and deal with the continued threat. Finally, the third stage is exhaustion, where we have been fighting off the perceived threat for too long and are now weakened. We get tired, lose our appetite, our immune system becomes suppressed, and we lose our motivation.

At least some of the long-term health consequences of stress have to do with the cortisol release during phase two. Cortisol is a hormone that increases metabolism and therefore provides additional fuel and improves your immune system in the short term. Over time, though, as a result of chronic stress, cortisol breaks down muscles and weakens the immune system. It causes weight gain, leads to trouble sleeping, increases blood pressure, and causes headaches. Long-term stress can also damage areas of the brain associated with memory and concentration.

Indeed, likely the result of this stress response and the role of cortisol, we see a broad spectrum of health consequences from chronic anger. It is not just the cardiovascular symptoms associated with Type A personality or found through the Precursors Study. Chronic anger has been tied to chronic pain, cancer, disease proneness, and arthritis. Some of this, though, is not explained purely by the direct impact of anger. There must be more going on than just the consequences of our fight-or-flight system and general adaptation syndrome.

As Smith pointed out in his 2006 analysis, it is likely that the impact of anger and hostility happens partly through more indirect mechanisms. Chronic anger may, for example, also impact our health through our health behaviors. Think for a moment about the myriad ways that people deal with negative emotions and stress. While there are some who handle it via more positive approaches like mediation and exercise, there are many who embrace a less healthy lifestyle during those difficult times. They may overeat, drink too much alcohol or smoke. They may get less sleep and less exercise. What we often find of the chronically angry is that they embrace a variety of these behaviors when they are mad, and those less healthy behaviors bring about negative health outcomes.

Take, for example, the 2000 study[36] by Drs. Linda Musante and Frank Treiber, who explored the relationship between anger-expression styles and health behaviors in teenagers. They surveyed more than 400 teenage participants, asking them questions about their anger and a variety of health behaviors (physical activity, alcohol and nicotine usage, and others). They found that anger-expression style did indeed influence health behaviors, with adolescents who suppressed their anger being less physically active and using alcohol more often. So here is a case where even a form of anger that is not always associated with physiological activation – because they are suppressing it instead of expressing it outwardly – still has a negative impact on physical health.

More than 20 stitches

One of the ways that anger can harm us physically, that we have not yet discussed, is likely the most obvious. Sometimes, we hurt ourselves – usually unintentionally but sometimes intentionally – as a result of our anger. I once had a client show me a laceration on her arm that had required more than 20 stitches. She said she got drunk the weekend before, got angry at her boyfriend, and punched a window. She broke the window and when she pulled her arm back through, she sliced it open on the glass still remaining in the window frame. As it stood, she was probably going to have permanent scars up and down her right arm. That said, she was actually quite lucky. She could have done far more damage to herself. She easily could have cut a major artery or done significant nerve damage. This was not the first time she had hurt herself when angry, but it was the worst time, and a signal to her that she needed some help.

This sort of unintentional self-harm can be a consequence for those with anger problems. They punch a wall and break their wrist. They kick a coffee table and break their foot. Compared with other consequences, the frequency of self-harm is low. According to our 2006[37] study, self-harm was easily the least common consequence, occurring about 0.17 times per month on average.* What is impossible to tease out from these findings, though, is how often these instances of self-harm are intentional. Some people will deal with their angry feelings through self-abuse. This speaks, quite honestly, to the complicated relationship anger has with other emotions like sadness, guilt, and jealousy.

Purely mad?

When I was first studying anger, my advisor and I were developing a mood-induction procedure. We wanted to elevate angry feelings in the lab, so we could study people *while* they were angry. Basically, we were creating a system for making people mad.† For some reason, it was important to members of my thesis committee that our anger induction only increased

---

* For comparison, problematic alcohol or other drug use was a consequence about 0.67 times per month.

† Granted, my friends and family would tell you that I have known how to make people mad since I was a kid, here I was trying to do it scientifically … in the laboratory … for research purposes.

anger and not other emotions. At the time, it made sense to me. We wanted to know how people act when they are angry – not scared, sad, jealous, or guilty – so we need them to be mad and *only* mad. We had them take a survey called the Differential Emotion Scale, which is just a series of five-inch lines, one for each feeling state, that they mark to indicate how they are feeling at that moment.* We had them take the survey, go through a mood induction, take the survey again, go through a different mood induction, then take the survey one final time.

We were mostly able to do it – make them really angry while just getting a little sad and scared, but it was difficult. We created a series of visualization procedures where participants were asked to imagine a frustrating situation happening to them. We landed on one where someone is bumped into, hard, at the grocery store without receiving an apology. As we worked on it, though, we found that a lot of people would get scared and sad too. This slowed us down, research-wise, because we had to keep revising the script to try and minimize those other emotions. In retrospect, I am not sure it made intuitive sense to care so much about trying to elevate purely anger. Outside of the lab, anger does not happen in a vacuum. People feel angry at the same time they get scared, sad, and jealous.

"Throwing things and yelling and crying"

This brings us to Chris,† a woman who shared with me how her angry outbursts are often tied to another emotion: anxiety.

My husband's favorite example was from our very first apartment that we were living in. I kept all my paperwork

---

* I remember that they were five inches because I had to measure each one with a ruler to determine their score. With nearly 300 participants and 12 measurements per participant, I made 3,600 measurements to determine how my participants were feeling at different stages of the study.

† Again, not her real name. Nor is Carl her husband's name.

and bills in these filing cabinet bins. They were these plastic bins with plastic lids on them. Well I got angry at him, and it was probably due to my anxiety. I don't even remember what the fight was about, but I picked up the lid of one of those bins and I flung it across the room. I was aiming for the wall. I was just so angry, and I threw it so hard that it shattered into a gajillion pieces. He loves telling that story, but for me it's so embarrassing.

It took me a long time to understand that I had anxiety and to realize what it was. And now I realize that my anxiety was where the anger was coming from. I think what was happening is that I was getting anxious and I wasn't able to think straight or accomplish anything or feel at ease. So then that would just make me feel angry because I wouldn't know what to do about it.

It just came out as anger whereas some people, they might sink into a depression or they might get overzealous and go crazy cleaning the house or whatever. For me, mine came out as anger and throwing things and yelling and crying.

I have generalized anxiety disorder and I get anxious about anything and everything. A lot of my anxiety used to be about driving a car especially. I would get anxious about coming up to a yellow light. Should I go through it or should I stop? Getting into trouble with the police was another one. Right now, I have very severe anxiety attacks about getting in trouble at work. Also, a lot of my anxiety extends to getting in trouble with Carl, my husband, even though I've never been in trouble with him before. Yeah, just like an overarching feeling of worry and anxiousness which are now controlled by medication thankfully.

The primary feature of generalized anxiety disorder (GAD) is *worry*. People with GAD worry about a variety of different things from making mistakes at work to terrible things happening to their loved ones. These negative thoughts flood their minds to the point that it is hard to focus, get things done, and sleep. For Chris, the pattern was to engage in this excessive worrying, get frustrated because of the impact it was having on her life, and lose her temper. She would feel out of control and that made her feel helpless, which led to feeling frustrated, angry and not knowing what to do about any of it.

I described this pattern for her and asked what she thought. Her response revealed a lot. "Yes," she said, "definitely. And then people would try and tell me *everything's okay* and *it's not a big deal,* and I would get angry."

People would try to help her, but they did it in a way that made her feel even worse. "They weren't listening to me," she said. "No one could understand, and I couldn't figure out how to express what I was feeling and they weren't getting it. Something was wrong and no one was paying attention to me."

Essentially, she was telling them she was scared, and in their rush to help her, they were unintentionally minimizing those feelings by telling her everything was going to be fine and to relax. It felt to her like they were telling her that her feelings were not real. Chris eventually went to therapy and got a better sense of what was going on.

"I would tell my therapist about how my least favorite words coming out of Carl's mouth were *everything's fine.* No everything's not fine! How are you not seeing the struggle going on in me? So now I'm learning through therapy proper techniques for how to articulate that struggle."

What Chris is describing is an important part of emotion management. People need to learn not just what they are feeling, but how to communicate those feelings to their loved ones. For Chris, she needed to learn to recognize when she was feeling anxious, tell her husband she was feeling anxious, but also help him understand how she felt when he unintentionally minimized those feelings.

"It started with a lot of recognizing that it was anxiety and accepting it," she told me. "That was the biggest thing. Just to accept that was what I was feeling. Trying to figure out what the triggers were – what was causing it? I also use a lot of grounding techniques, but my favorite one is the five senses where first you think of five things you can see, four things you can touch, three things you can hear, two things you can smell, one thing you can taste. By the time you get down to that one thing you've kind of distracted your mind from the anxiety and you're focused on the things that are tangible."

A secondary emotion?

Chris's story is not terribly unusual. In fact, I am routinely asked if I believe anger is a *secondary emotion*.* In fact, I was once asked on a job interview "Was Yoda right?"

"About?" I asked.

"When he said 'Fear leads to anger. Anger leads to hate. Hate leads to suffering.' Was he right?" He went on to say that he felt like people got angry when they lost something or when they might lose something and that the natural response to loss or potential loss was sadness or fear, respectively.

I understand his argument, and I think that sometimes it is true. Sometimes we lose something – a loved one dies or we lose a meaningful job – and we are sad first. But that sadness might turn to anger as we process the loss. We become angry over the circumstances that led to the loved one's death. We become angry at the boss who fired us, or the poor economy that led to our dismissal. There is a similar argument out there that anger is really just depression turned outward. When people have anger problems, they are really just depressed and do not know how to deal with it.

---

* I am not always asked. Sometimes I am just told, like the guy who called into a radio show I was a guest on and said (with some hostility), "I will remind the good doctor that anger is a secondary emotion that comes from fear and sadness." It felt presumptuous. How does he know if I am a good doctor?

I am less sensitive to the latter argument. Depression has a clinical definition according the *DSM-5*, and is largely defined as either feelings of intense sadness or decreased pleasure. There are nine different symptoms of depression and the closest any of them gets to feelings of anger is that sometimes depressed children become irritable. Those who think of anger as "depression turned outward" are using a different definition of depression than the rest of the field.

In my view, anger is not inherently *secondary* to any other emotions. However, in a particular circumstance, it might be secondary. The grief examples above are certainly cases where anger is secondary to those emotions. I had a client who was suffering from severe post-traumatic stress disorder following a combat-related plane crash he was involved in. His initial response was intense fear, but over time that fear turned into anger toward anyone and everyone involved in the crash. As I said before, emotions are complicated. They typically do not happen on their own and we respond to life events with a variety of different feelings.

There are a number of reasons why this happens. First, for some it might be a coping mechanism. Think for a moment – if you got to choose, would you rather feel scared, sad, or angry? Chances are, given those options, you would choose anger. Quite simply, it feels less negative than these other emotions. It is likely that some people, when they are feeling sad or scared, reappraise situations in a way that make them feel less uncomfortable. They are not lying to themselves so much as they start to focus on the parts of the situation that lead them to get mad rather than sad or scared.

For example, I had a client who suffered a break-in where someone stole her television. They did it in the middle of the night when she was home, asleep in the other room. She had no idea until the next morning when she woke up to an open window in her family room and a missing television. At first, she was shocked and scared. "How could this happen?" she asked herself. "How could someone break into my house in the middle of the night without me even knowing?" It made her feel vulnerable. "They could have attacked me," she said to me. "They could have raped me." Quickly, though, she moved on to the parts of this situation that made her angry. She shifted her focus from the fear to the anger. "And now I don't have a TV. I've got to buy a new television because some asshole came and stole my stuff."

It is not unlike looking away from a scary part in a movie or saying "It's fine" when something is deeply saddening to you. I have a good friend who routinely says "It's all good" when things are clearly not all good. For him, it is a coping mechanism. What he is really saying is "I do not want to feel this right now, so I am reframing it as less sad." The client above did not wish to think about her vulnerability. She wanted to feel empowered, and her anger at the thief made her feel powerful instead of vulnerable.

Overlapping thought types

The other link in these emotions, though, goes back to the reasons why we get angry in the first place. As you know, anger emerges as an interplay between a precipitant, the pre-anger state, and the appraisal of that precipitant. Ultimately, part of this appraisal process is not just to determine if you should be angry, but to determine if you should be scared or saddened by the stimulus (whether you interpret the stimulus as a threat or a loss). Plus, those thoughts we have that lead to anger – some of them also lead to fear and sadness. Catastrophizing, for example, is a core thought associated with fear and anxiety. If you interpret an event as the worst thing that has ever happened, you will likely get scared as well as angry.

This is one of the things I investigated when I built the Angry Cognitions Scale – the questionnaire that measured those five angry thought types (overgeneralizing, demandingness, misattributing causation, catastrophizing, and inflammatory labeling). I wanted to know whether or not those thoughts predicted anxiety and depression too. I gave my participants a scale called the Depression Anxiety Stress Scales (DASS)[38] and looked for relationships between catastrophizing, overgeneralizing and so on and those other feeling states.

Indeed, they were related. Not only is anger heavily correlated with both sadness and anxiety, which I have found in just about every study where I have asked that question, but each of these feeling states was correlated with these negative thought types too. Another study we did in 2005[39] using a different questionnaire – the Cognitive Emotion Regulation Questionnaire – found that thoughts related to catastrophizing and rumination were related with depression, anxiety, and anger. This study even found that blaming others, a thought type we usually assume to be heavily related to anger, was just as relevant to anxiety as it was to anger. Even though these feeling states are quite different from each other, their thoughts and physiologies are similar.

ACTIVITY: ANGER, SADNESS, AND/OR FEAR

For this activity, I want you to revisit one of the angry incidents you diagramed earlier and ask yourself how much of your response was anger and how much something else? Were you *purely* angry, or were you also feeling sadness, fear, jealousy, or some other emotion?

Next, if you were feeling some other emotion, what do you think was driving those feelings? Was your anger the result of you focusing on the angering parts to feel more powerful? Was it that the thoughts you were having (such as catastrophizing, blaming others) also lead to other feelings besides anger?

Not always rational

Of course, these thoughts we have when we are angry are not always rational. We have likely all been in situations where we have been so angry that we thought or even said something we later realized did not make much sense. We may have even embarrassed ourselves by doing something we later regretted – something deeply irrational.

CHAPTER 9

IRRATIONAL THINKING

Caught on video

YouTube is littered with videos of people losing their temper. People send them to me all the time – sometimes friends and coworkers, just for fun and to get my thoughts, and sometimes news media because they want a comment on what is going on from an anger perspective. "Check this out, anger guy! Can you believe it?" they write along with link to a video of a woman standing on the side of the road calling 911 because someone gave her the finger or there is a man threatening someone with a bat over a bill dispute. There are a few different versions of these videos. Some are security footage that catch some sort of dispute on the road or in a store. Some are captured by news media covering an event where an argument breaks out. Lately, though, most seem to be arguments among strangers in public where one person takes out a phone part way through to record the incident.

I appreciate watching these videos because they offer a glimpse into something I do not actually get to see very often. People tell me their anger stories all the time, but I rarely get to see them firsthand. These videos offer a look at how people think and behave when they are really angry. Almost by definition, we are dealing with extreme rage in these videos. Otherwise, most of them would not have been recorded in the first place and certainly would not have gone viral.

By and large, these videos show enraged people expressing their anger outwardly, either through physical aggression or verbal aggression. They include yelling, screaming, threats of violence, obscene language, or even actual acts of physical aggression. I have already addressed anger-motivated violence in chapter 6 but want to explore something different here that I have always been fascinated by. Something that these videos show in ways we do not often get to witness is that when people are truly enraged, they will say odd and often even nonsensical things.

"I'll take you down"

Take, for example, a 2018 video of a parking dispute in a store parking lot. The general issue seemed to be that a woman thought the man who parked next to her parked too close to her car. The video starts after she has already expressed some anger, but the description (written by the man who parked next to her and recorded the video) indicates that she parked first and he parked moments later. According to the description, she became angry with him for parking too close so he adjusted his car and started the video when he got out of the car to capture the rest of the incident.

In this two-minute video, she goes on a solid one-minute largely uninterrupted rant. She swears at him repeatedly, calls him an "old fart," tells him he's too old to drive a car that big, accuses him of having a small penis and suggests he drives a big car to make up for it, asks if he receives sexual gratification by arguing with a woman, and challenges him to a physical fight. The video ends with her saying "I'll take you down, you son of a bitch ... anytime" – and then she turns around and walks into the store. The man recording the video certainly eggs her on with sarcastic comments and other jokes at her expense, but based on what we see in the video and how others in the video are responding to the situation, this is an extraordinary overreaction.

What is really something, though, is that when it comes to what seems to be the precipitant here – his having parked close to her – she seems to be the one in the wrong. The evidence is right there in the video. She is parked over the line on his car's side of her spot. His car does appear to be enormous and barely fits between the lines of the parking spot, but if one of them parked poorly in this instance, at least after he readjusted, it was her. This is pointed out to her by both the man she is arguing with and another person in the parking lot. You can see a man in the background pointing out to her that she is parked too far over. She appears to snap at him too, but you cannot hear what she says to him. She is simply too angry to admit that she might not have parked as well as she originally thought.

What is interesting to me is that the evidence is clear enough that a person in a rational state of mind would be able to see it.* A person who is thinking clearly would be able to look at this and at least say to themselves, "Even though he should have parked farther away from me, this is largely my mistake." So why does she not see it? That is just it, though. Often, when people are in a fit of rage they are no longer thinking rationally. The same impulse control issues that we talked about in chapter 6 as leading to violence will sometimes lead to absurd and irrational fits and tirades, including statements that people later realize were unreasonable and regret.

The problem for me in evaluating these videos, though, is that I rarely get to know the backstory. Even in this case where I think we get to see most of the interaction, some things happened before the video started that likely drove the anger. Even when I can get a sense for why they are arguing

---

* I am going to take a moment to say, I know there will be other interpretations of this video. Much like the airplane example from chapter 4, there are "unwritten rules" about parking. I certainly do not know all these unwritten rules but I bet there are people out there who think you should never park next to someone who just parked or that if you have a large car, you should park at the end of a row when possible.

or what led to the dispute, I rarely know anything about the people involved. What I want is a sense of what they are typically like. Is this rant part of a pattern? Or was this a one-off singular event where they lost their cool? Maybe they even regretted it later? There is no way of knowing if we are witnessing an otherwise rational person whose anger led to a fit of irrational thinking or a person who behaves and thinks this way all the time.*

Mood-induced irrationality

For a long time, I have been really curious about the nonsense that people, including myself on occasion, express when really angry. This was something I would witness from my dad fairly often, the most extreme version, though, when I was about ten years old. I was sitting in the back seat of his car. He was driving, his wife (my parents divorced when I was young and he remarried) was in the passenger seat, and we were leaving a restaurant in downtown Minneapolis. It was a weekend night and the Minnesota Twins, the professional baseball team, had just finished a game. We had not gone to the game but we were close to the stadium so were dealing with the traffic, both driving and pedestrian. I could tell my dad was starting to get agitated,† and it was making me uncomfortable. He started raising his voice every time someone did something he

---

* There are a handful of instances where the ranter has been identified and we have got hold of a follow-up interview. There have been mixed results in these instances. Chris Reichert, who was caught on video in 2010 yelling and throwing money at a man with Parkinson's disease, apologized a few days later and said he "snapped." Daniel Maples, who went on a tirade over being asked to wear a mask at a store that required them because of the COVID-19 pandemic, implied that the video did not show the "real" him, but did not apologize and said there was more to the story than what was seen on the video.

† It interesting to me how angry he was at the people around him. I get the frustration (goal-blocking), but if this happened to me I would likely be more angry with myself than with others. Why did I come downtown for dinner on a game night?

disliked. He started talking to the other drivers as if they could hear him: "Oh you're not pulling out in front of me! No way! It's my turn!"

We were stopped at a red light with literally thousands of pedestrians around us. When the light turned green for us, there were still people crossing the street in front of us even though they now had a "Don't Walk" signal. My dad rolled down his window and started to yell things like "You've got a red light" and "Get out of the road." His wife looked back at me and smirked as if to say "Uh oh, he's doing it again." His temper was a running joke with many, even me, though I do not think I realized at the time how scary I found it. I tried to sink into the upholstery of the back seat, feeling embarrassed and nervous.

Even if the situation was a little bit funny so far, it quickly lost any humor. He started to rev his engine and inch forward. I am confident he was not trying to hurt anyone. He just wanted to signal that it was his turn and people should stop crossing the road. He scared one of the walkers, though, and a man crossing in front of us pushed the woman he was with out of the way and sat on the front of my dad's car. Instead of stopping, my dad started to pull forward even faster and drove nearly 20 feet with this stranger sitting on the hood. The woman this man had pushed out of the way started yelling in our open window, "You son of a bitch. I'm pregnant!" to which my dad replied by slamming on the brakes, causing the man to slide off the front of the car, and yelling "If you're pregnant you should stay out of the road."

In this fit of frustration, he yelled at people, revved his engine at them, drove with a person on the hood of his car, and told a pregnant woman that she should stay out of the road. I was horrified, certain I was going to witness a serious fight. While this was certainly an excessive example, this is the sort of thing that would happen sometimes. A normally very smart person would say and do wildly irrational things when he was mad. He would get impatient and say something ridiculous. "They don't sell gum at the airport," he once told me as we walked to our gate to wait for a flight. He was frustrated by how long security had taken and did not want to stop.* Another time he only wanted dessert at a restaurant and the waiter told us we needed to order a full meal if we wanted a seat (there was a long wait). My dad *yelled* at him, "We've been here before and didn't get dessert, so we're just coming to get that dessert now!"

It is not just him that has made me so curious about this. I routinely talk to clients who describe things they cannot believe they said when they were angry. One told me she got angry and ran away from her friends at a bar one night and then called them screaming that they should have chased after her. Another threatened to sue a fast-food restaurant for running out of her favorite sandwich. Similarly, people routinely displace frustration that probably should be directed at themselves onto inanimate objects. "Where did those damn car keys go?" people will ask, as though the keys are responsible for the fact that you misplaced them. There is even some research that says that people who typically identify as atheists will somehow become angry at God when they experience significant losses.[40] So a question I have long wondered about is what makes people, especially otherwise smart people, think and say such irrational things when they are angry?

Unfortunately, the research literature on this is not that helpful to me. Searches for "irrationality" and "irrational thinking" are mostly tied up in a different topic that has been well researched: irrational beliefs. I mentioned irrational beliefs earlier, in chapter 4, when I was discussing the role of appraisal in why we get mad. These beliefs are a core element of rational emotive behavior therapy (REBT), an emotion therapy approach developed by Dr. Albert Ellis. These irrational

---

* This is the sort of trick you try with a small child. "Sorry, but it looks like they are out of ice-cream." But I was a teenager. That trick does not work with a teenager. Obviously, I knew they sold gum at the airport.

beliefs are essentially core values that drive our interpretation of events in the world ("It is completely horrible when I am treated poorly. If I make a mistake, I am a complete failure"). This is a very different type of irrationality than I am interested in right now. This type of irrational thinking causes anger (event happens, we view it through the lens of our irrational belief, and we get mad). What I am interested in is what irrational things we think *when* we get angry that we might not think otherwise.

Here is the study I was hoping to find: One where the participants were made to be angry via some sort of mood induction, maybe a visualization procedure like we used in those early studies. You get them good and mad and then ask them to describe their thoughts about the situation. This is called the "articulated thoughts in simulated situations paradigm" and it allows for researchers to get a sense of the thoughts people have in particular situations. It has been used to explore reactions to intimate partner violence, effectiveness of therapeutic approaches, and even reactions to hate crimes. It has received very little attention, however, with regard to anger.

That said, just recently in 2018, Dr. Erica Birkley and Christopher Eckhardt[41] used this approach to study emotion regulation related to intimate partner violence. Their study is not exactly what I am curious about (for example, exploring the irrational thinking that emerges when angry), but it is as close as I can get in the published research. They asked participants to imagine one of two scenarios, one in which they overhear their romantic partner flirting with someone and one in which they overhear their partner having an emotionally neutral conversation with someone. The former has been shown to induce anger and jealousy and the latter was designed to be neutral and in this case to serve as a control. Participants were asked to "talk out loud" during predetermined breaks in the scenario. Those statements were recorded and coded into one of three categories: verbal aggression, physical aggression, and belligerence (statements that were threatening or "designed to entice an altercation").

They were particularly interested in the impact different emotion-regulation strategies might have on those articulated thoughts. Participants were taught to manage their emotions in particular ways prior to the study and asked to use those approaches when provoked. They found that those participants who had been instructed in cognitive reappraisal – to reconsider the thoughts they are having – were less likely to have aggressive articulations when angry. In other words, participants who had been taught and encouraged to think about their thoughts and to modify them while angry were less likely to articulate violent statements.

This study is important for two reasons. First, it demonstrates what could be a valuable method in better understanding the thoughts, irrational or otherwise, that people have in moments of intense anger. It is not perfect – no research method ever is – but it could give us some understanding. Second, it shows how reappraisal can be a valuable approach to minimizing those aggressive thoughts. This is something we will talk about extensively later in the book.

Given the absence of research on irrational thinking *while angry*, we mostly have to guess at what is going on here. There are really two things that are likely playing a role. The first has to do with impulse control and our prefrontal cortex. As you already know from chapter 3, our prefrontal cortex is responsible for impulse control. It is the part of our brain that keeps us from doing or saying things we might *want* to do or say. It is also the part of our brain that takes care of planning, organizing, and decision-making. When people feel things, this is the part of our brain that decides what we do with those feelings. The thing we have not yet talked about, though, is how for some this part of the brain might be less active when they are angry. They are not missing part of it, the way Phineas Gage was after the explosion, but they may as well be as it is not doing the work of impulse control.

Again, the study I would like to read on this does not exist yet. Ideally, we would do an fMRI (functional magnetic resonance imaging) on someone while they are being provoked to see how the prefrontal cortex responds. Perhaps we would ask them to either suppress their desire to lash out or act on that desire by aggressing in some way. We could then make comparisons between what happens in the brain when people suppress or express their anger. Alternatively, we could ask them to articulate their thoughts while being provoked and look for relationships between brain activity and particularly unreasonable or irrational statements. We might discover that those who articulate especially irrational thoughts see less activity in their prefrontal cortex when angry. Those might be the people who try to convince their teenage sons that they do not sell gum at the airport.

There is a recent study that can give us some insight into this. Also in 2018, this one, conducted by Dr. Gadi Gilam and his research team,[42] explored how people made monetary decisions when provoked. Participants played an "anger-infused ultimatum game" where they were made monetary offers that were allegedly, though not really, coming from previous participants. The offers were either fair, medium, or unfair and were accompanied by a statement from the non-existent previous participant. Statements were either non-hostile ("Let's split it equally"), moderately hostile ("That's the offer, deal with it"), or quite hostile ("Come on, loser!!!"). Though they were taught the game in advance, participants actually played the game in an fMRI scanner so the researchers could study the activity of their prefrontal cortex while being made the offers. They found that the unfair/angering condition (getting an unfair offer while being called a "loser") led to increased activity in the prefrontal cortex. Arguably, the prefrontal cortex has to do additional work to deal with that anger.

This study is already fascinating, but there is another element that makes it really extraordinary. At the same time that they were playing the game, they were having part of their brain stimulated via a "weak electrical current," which as we know from some of the studies discussed in chapter 3 can influence brain activity. They found that they were actually able to influence the acceptance of unfair offers by stimulating the prefrontal cortex. Essentially, stimulating the cortex led to decreased feelings of anger, which led to an increase in accepting unfair offers. Why would this be? Well, it speaks to the protective nature of anger. The anger we feel when we are treated unfairly prevents us from making bad decisions. When you decrease that anger, there is nothing there to protect us.

On the surface, this runs counter to the point of the chapter, that anger can make you do and say irrational things. Why does anger help in this instance? The thing to keep in mind here is that the anger experienced in this study is relatively minor. The participants were called "losers" and offered an unfair monetary deal. That obviously is not very nice and should probably make you mad, but it is not the same as some of the provocations people encounter in their life outside of the lab.

What would happen if we could do a study like this but induce far more intense anger?* Perhaps we might find that the prefrontal cortex's capacity to manage rational decisions is overrun by the strength of the emotion. People start doing and saying things they do not truly *believe*† because the part of brain responsible for stopping them has been minimized.

Perhaps there is another way of getting at this question. Could we possibly *shut down* the prefrontal cortex of a well-functioning brain, induce anger, and see how the person

---

* I hope it goes without saying that we should not do this for ethical reasons, but just in case it does not go without saying, I am saying it: We should not do this for ethical reasons.

† You could really go down a rabbit hole here. On some level we must "believe" these irrational statements, right? We said them. We can decide later that we do not really agree with it, but it is not as though it came from nowhere. Ultimately, it came from our brain. Maybe a different part of our brain, but still our brain.

responds? Indeed, we can, so-to-speak, via a popular drug called … alcohol, which has well-known effects on the prefrontal cortex. Decision-making, working memory, planning, and so on are all impacted by alcohol. So, what happens when scientists get people drunk and induce anger? Those people get aggressive.

Dr. Eckhardt (the same scientist as above) answered this question in 2008[43] by putting participants in one of two groups: alcohol or placebo. After consuming the alcoholic drink that had been prepared for them, they participated in the "articulated thoughts in simulated situations" task (similar to above). They listened to a recorded description of an angering situation, and they voiced their thoughts into a microphone as they had them. Again, their thoughts were coded as verbal aggression, physical aggression, and belligerence. They found that people who had (a) scored high on an aggressiveness questionnaire and (b) were randomly assigned to get an alcoholic drink were eight times more likely to make aggressive statements when provoked than any other group. Most interesting to this topic, though, is that they were three times more likely to vocalize aggressive thoughts than those who scored high on an aggressiveness questionnaire but did not get a drink.

What does this tell us? Well, it says that decreasing the impact of the prefrontal cortex really does matter when it comes to anger control. When it is minimized, we voice aggressive statements we otherwise would not. What it does not tell us is whether or not an otherwise rational person could have their prefrontal cortex overrun by anger alone to say and do profoundly irrational things.

Rationalizing irrational positions

I think there is another piece of this puzzle, though, above and beyond the activity of different parts of the brain. I suspect that when some people are angry they feel an even greater need to be right. To serve that need, they are willing to do all sorts of intellectual gymnastics and make all sorts of cognitive leaps. If telling someone they deserve to be served dessert tonight for all the times they have not had dessert in the past will win them the argument in their mind, they will go for it. If verbally attacking the person they think parked too closely to them and labeling them in all sorts of obscene ways allows them to more easily ignore the fact that they were actually the one who parked poorly, they do it.

We can think of this as a version of cognitive dissonance, a concept described by Dr. Leon Festinger in his 1957 book *A Theory of Cognitive Dissonance*. Essentially, when people's behaviors are inconsistent with their beliefs, they become uncomfortable (they experience dissonance). As Festinger describes it: "The existence of dissonance, being psychologically uncomfortable, will motivate the person to try and reduce the dissonance and achieve consonance."* In other words, the solution to that dissonance is often to justify the behavior by tweaking the thoughts and beliefs. Imagine, for example, someone who purports that one of their fundamental values is that they care about the environment. They receive new information, though, when they learn that raising livestock is a major contributor to environmental destruction. As a meat eater, they can either change their behavior and stop eating meat or change their belief system. Instead of changing their behavior, people often shift their belief systems from something like "It is everyone's responsibility to protect the environment in whatever way they can" to "People should take

---

* The second part of his hypothesis is equally important, but less relevant here: "When dissonance is present, in addition to trying to reduce it the person will actively avoid situations and information which would likely increase the dissonance." In other words, people will avoid information that makes them uncomfortable so their beliefs are never challenged. We see this play out globally with political discussions and the sources of information they seek. But we also see it play out interpersonally with the conversations people have. If asking someone how you made them feel makes you uncomfortable, you might just not ask them.

reasonable steps to protect the environment." That subtle shift in thinking allows them to feel comfortable caring about the environment while enjoying a steak every now and then.

How does this apply to the irrational thoughts and behaviors people might engage in when they are really angry? It makes people uncomfortable to feel like they are in the wrong or have made a mistake, especially if they hold a core value or belief that it is important to always be right. When they overreact or are in the wrong, cognitive dissonance theory suggests they need to adjust their thinking in order to feel more comfortable. Like the meat eater above, they modify their thoughts so that they feel like they behaved reasonably or that their angry response was justified.

To revisit the parking lot rant example above, the situation was at least partly the angry ranter's fault. She was the person who parked poorly. Yet, rather than own that mistake, which might have made her feel vulnerable and increased feelings of dissonance, she externalized things toward the other driver. She made the cause of the problem that he drives "too big" a car, invented reasons why he drives such a big car, and ignored all evidence to the contrary (avoiding information that increases feelings of dissonance).

ACTIVITY: THE MOST ANGRY YOU HAVE EVER BEEN

For this activity, I want you to think about the most angry you have ever been. Then, focus on the thoughts you had – not the ones that led to your anger, but the ones you had once you were angry.

1   Think about the most angry you have ever been.
2   What did you think, say, and do? Was it reasonable? Were you thinking clearly?
3   Was there conflict between your core values and what you had done (that is, were you experiencing cognitive dissonance)?
4   What does this reveal about your core values?

Evaluating consequences

Obviously, people can experience a number of consequences as a result of their anger. From health problems – both mental and physical – to damaged relationships, anger can easily interfere in our lives. It can lead to violent interactions and other sorts of impulsive behaviors that can harm us or those around us. Plus, when we are angry we may embarrass ourselves by saying and doing thoughtless and irrational things.

At the same time, though, it is through these problems that we might learn to better understand ourselves. An evaluation of our anger in relationships can reveal important information about what we value. The irrational things we do or say when we are mad can tell us about our core beliefs. We just have to be willing to unpack those things more deeply. We will explore this and more in part three.

PART THREE

HEALTHY ANGER

CHAPTER 10

UNDERSTANDING ANGER

Catastrophic conditions

When I was 26 years old, I was driving to my first ever professional conference presentation. It was the American Psychological Association Annual Convention in Chicago, and I was presenting my masters thesis. It was a big deal for me, and I was both excited and nervous. I was staying a bit outside of the city at my brother's house, so I had about an hour-long drive into town the morning of my presentation. I do not like being late for things – or even feeling rushed – so I got up early and left the house with what I thought was plenty of time.

What I did not know is that there had been heavy rain in the city the night before. Some of the downtown Chicago area was flooded, and they had closed a few of the streets. Traffic was terrible and what would have been a 60-minute drive was looking to be much longer than that. It became clear early on in the commute that even though I had given myself about two hours to get there, I would be lucky to make it for the start of my presentation.

I started to get really frustrated. Anger over weather is particularly interesting because there is no obvious perpetrator.

There is no culprit, no villain to be angry at.* But that did not stop me from getting agitated. I was alone in the car, but started to yell every now and then at no one in particular; just shouting at the heavens. About one hour into what ended up being a drive taking two hours and fifteen minutes,† I realized I needed to calm down. I literally said to myself, "Okay, Ryan, you're on your way to give a presentation on why people get angry. Maybe use some of that psychology on yourself right now."

So I stopped externalizing things and started thinking about how I was feeling. Not just the thoughts I was having, but the entire picture. The traffic (the precipitant), my mood leading into it (my pre-anger state), and the thoughts I was having (my appraisal). I realized something very obvious first, that this was no one's fault. It was the result of bad weather, and even if I felt like some other drivers were making the problem worse, they were just trying to do the same thing as me – make it to their destination. They probably had important things to get to as well, some likely much more important than my presentation.

I also realized that what was driving my anger as much as anything was the nervousness I was feeling about the conference. If we removed that part of the equation, it was still frustrating to be stuck in traffic for that long, but it was not nearly as bad. In fact, from a pre-anger-state perspective, there were a lot of things working against me. I had slept poorly the night before because I was nervous. I had not eaten very much that morning to save time. I was wearing a suit, which is less comfortable for me than other clothes. Each of these is relatively minor on its own,

---

* This is true for quite a few provocations related to natural disasters. When big events have to be cancelled because of rain, a snowstorm leads to a car accident, or a virus causes an international health crisis with widespread physical-health, mental-health, and economic consequences, people get angry and do not always know who or what to be angry with.

† For those of you doing the math, this made me fifteen minutes late for my presentation.

but collectively they make a difference. I was tired, hungry, anxious, and physically uncomfortable.

But what was most revealing to me was how I was appraising the situation. When we revisit those five types of thoughts (misattributing causation, overgeneralizing, demandingness, catastrophizing, and inflammatory labeling), one stands out in particular. I was catastrophizing. Sure, there was a little bit of each of these mixed in. I found myself getting mad at the other drivers (misattributing causation) and calling them idiots (inflammatory labeling). I caught myself saying things like "this sort of thing always happens to me" (overgeneralizing) and even feeling a little bit entitled (demandingness). But what was worse than all of those thoughts was that I had decided that this was going to ruin my career.

I kept running through the consequences of being late to my presentation, and in my head they were disastrous. This was going to be publicly embarrassing. I was going to offend people who I may want to work for some day. Dr. Jerry Deffenbacher, the researcher I mentioned in chapter 2, was going to be there, and he would be disappointed in me. He might tell my advisor, so I would hear about it from him too. Worse yet, what if I was not just late? What if I missed the entire thing? I would have done all this work and come to Chicago for a presentation, only to miss the entire thing and embarrass myself.

When I stopped myself from catastrophizing and took time to actually think about the thoughts I was having, I forced myself to work through the most likely scenarios and what they would actually mean to my career. First, I was probably not going to miss the entire presentation. I was probably just going to be late. That would be embarrassing to me, but people would likely understand given the weather. My advisor might be disappointed in me, but hopefully he too would understand (especially as I am not frequently late to things). The same could be said for meeting Dr. Deffenbacher.

Hopefully, he would understand.* Ultimately, when I stopped and evaluated each thought I was having, I realized that most of my catastrophic ones were not that likely to come true. The situation was far from ideal, but it was unlikely to be disastrous.

This is one of the ways we can deal with our anger, by better understanding where it is coming from. The value of developing such understanding was explored in a 2017 article on the role of emotional intelligence with regard to anger and aggression.[44] Garcia-Sancho and colleagues gave more than 650 participants a test of their emotional intelligence. It measured how good those participants were at perceiving, using, managing, and understanding their emotions. It is important to note that this was a test that measured their ability to do these things, with correct and incorrect answers. Some research on emotional intelligence uses self-report measures with items like, on a scale of one to five, how easy it is for others to confide in you? Such indicators are not going to be very valuable. As everyone knows, you can think you are good at something and not actually be very good at it.†

What they found was that emotional intelligence, overall, was negatively correlated with anger, physical aggression, verbal aggression, and passive aggression. The more emotionally wise you were, the less likely you were to feel angry or become aggressive. In fact, the authors state that "These findings suggest that having high emotional skills can reduce the risk of being physically aggressive and explain why not all individuals with higher levels of trait anger engage frequently in physical

---

* A funny side-note here is that when I got to the conference and met Dr. Deffenbacher (who I was meeting for the first time), I was obsequiously apologetic. He stopped me and said, "It's really not a big deal. I just got here a few minutes ago."

† For comparison's sake, imagine if we tried to measure general intelligence this way. Instead of asking a specific question like "What is the capital of Mexico?" with correct and incorrect answers, we would ask "On a scale of one to five, how well do you know the geography of Mexico?"

aggression." In other words, one of the reasons why angry people are not always aggressive people is because they are also able to understand, manage, and use their anger in healthy ways.

Ultimately, it all goes back to the model we discussed in chapter 2. To be able to honestly evaluate the three elements (precipitant, pre-anger state, and appraisal) can help you have a healthier emotional life.

Should we be angry?

First, evaluating why we are angry can help us answer a really important question: Should we be angry? I want to be clear from the outset that the question "Should we be angry?" is obviously a judgment. There is no formula we can use to determine if we *should* be angry in a given situation. There is, however, a series of questions we can ask ourselves to help us determine (a) if we should be mad and (b) how mad we should be. They are:

1 Was I treated poorly, unfairly, or otherwise wronged?
2 Is someone or something blocking my goals?
3 What might I have done to contribute to this?

Let us go through each of these questions and talk about how to answer them. First, and perhaps the easiest, were you treated poorly or wronged? The reason I believe this is the easiest is because the answer is probably *yes*. Remember from the discussion of evolution in chapter 3, the reason anger exists in the first place is because it alerts us to the fact that we have been wronged or treated unfairly. Chances are that those angry feelings are your brain's way of communicating that someone is treating you poorly. Take time still, though, and ask yourself this question from an unbiased a perspective as possible.

In the example above about the traffic in Chicago, I was actually not being treated poorly or unfairly. Though it felt personal because it was such an important day for me, in reality, I was suffering through the same set of circumstances as everyone else in Chicago. So the answer to question one was actually a *no* this time. That said, the answer to the second question, is someone or something blocking my goals, was an unequivocal *yes*. I had a very clear and simple goal, to get to this event on time, and the weather was interfering in my completion of that goal. What makes this a really valuable question, though, is it helps people to think about possible solutions. If you know your goals are being blocked and that is why you are angry, a natural follow-up is to start thinking about what to do about it.

Now we get to the toughest question, because it requires a level of self-reflection and honesty that is difficult for many people – and can be nearly impossible for people *when* they are angry. When you ask yourself "What might I have done to contribute to this?" you are essentially asking "Is it possible I started this, did I intentionally or unintentionally do something that led to this, and are they right to be treating me this way?" Those are not necessarily fun questions to ask yourself because they require an admission of guilt and the corresponding feelings of guilt. They also include a sense of vulnerability that we already acknowledged in the previous chapter is hard to admit to and feel in a moment of anger.

That said, this is probably the most important of these three questions. As was mentioned in chapter 7, anger is a social emotion. We usually feel it in the context of an interaction with another human being, and we have to acknowledge that we bring something to those interactions. We need to consider how something we said or did may have influenced the situation. Sometimes it is going to be obvious. We said something intentionally hurtful and they responded by treating us similarly poorly. Often, though, it will be less obvious. Maybe we unintentionally hurt their feelings, maybe our overall approach to the situation was something that put them on edge from the start.

Imagine, for example, you have a meeting at work that you are absolutely dreading. You have had bad experiences with this person in the past and you expect this to be another one of those bad experiences. As you get closer and closer to the meeting you find yourself running through all the different things this person will probably say to you and you find yourself getting increasingly agitated. By the time the meeting rolls around, you are at a point where you expect the worst, and you approach the meeting with an undercurrent of hostility and frustration. Even though you do not voice this frustration directly, it is present in your facial expressions, tone, posture, and overall demeanor. This visible agitation will likely influence how the other person interacts with you and it may lead to some agitation from them that would not have been there otherwise.

This way that people sometimes "unintentionally elicit predictable reactions from others in their social environment" is what social psychologist Dr. David Buss refers to as "evocation."[45] Essentially, competitive people tend to elicit competitiveness from others. Irritable people elicit irritability from people. They approach people expecting those people to be rude to them, so they are rude first, and unintentionally elicit rudeness in response.

A related concept from the literature that is more specific to anger is what Dr. Jerry Deffenbacher referred to as *overestimation* and *underestimation*. He writes that "angry individuals tend to overestimate the probability of negative events."[46] We actually tried to write items for this tendency to misestimate probabilities when we wrote the Angry Cognitions Scale. As it turns out, though, these types of thoughts are so highly contextual – so situation specific – that it was nearly impossible to write meaningful items to capture it.

What we know is that when we are about to engage in an activity that we anticipate will be unpleasant, we overestimate the likelihood that it will go poorly. You go on a trip, but instead of being excited about the destination, you spend the morning envisioning long lines at the airport and travel delays. By the time you get there, you are so certain it will be frustrating that you have made yourself angry in the lead up to it. Even if things go relatively smoothly, two things have happened. First, you made yourself angry anyway. Second, when relatively small things do go wrong, you interpret them through the lens of "See, I knew it was going to go wrong" and you become more angry than you otherwise would over a relatively small thing.

All of this is to suggest that there are times we unintentionally play a role in how other people treat us. This is not to suggest that we *deserve* to be treated poorly or anything like that, but to say that we contribute to the social situations that we find ourselves in, and sometimes we do things – either intentionally or unintentionally – that lead to the treatment we receive from others. As we search to understand our anger, we need to be honest about this piece of the puzzle.

What does my anger tell me about the situation?

As you know by now, anger emerges from this interaction between a precipitant, our mood at the time of that precipitant (the pre-anger state), and our interpretation or appraisal. You can diagram just about every anger episode using this model. Such diagrams are really useful ways to better understand the specific situation you are in and why you are feeling the way you are feeling. This is what I did above as I was delayed in driving to that conference. I thought about each element of the model and assessed as honestly and unbiasedly as I could what was going on.

When we do this sort of assessment, it helps us manage our anger differently (which we will address more fully in the next chapter), but it also helps us better understand the situation we are in, the people we are interacting with, and the outcome we are hoping for. By evaluating why we are feeling the way we are feeling, we come out of the situation with a better understanding of what is happening and what we want from it.

This also takes the onus of responsibility off the instigator or provocation and allows you to consider the bigger picture, including your own role. On the surface, that may sound like it would make things worse. One might think, "So, by understanding the incident better I can see how I'm partly responsible. Won't that just make me feel guilty or sad?" While I can see how those feelings could emerge,* it can actually be really empowering to recognize the role you play in angering situations because that is the part of the situation you can change.

Let us revisit an example from chapter 2, the woman who would routinely become frustrated about the drop-off line at her kids' school. By way of reminder, she had strong opinions about how parents *should* act in the drop-off line when taking her kids to school. These were largely unwritten rules that she followed rather than anything prescribed by the school. She felt they were "common sense" but others obviously did not see it that way. When evaluating this angering event using Deffenbacher's model, you can see how the provocation stays largely the same but the other elements change. Some of her anger emerged from her pre-anger state – feeling rushed on her way to work. Some of it emerged from her evaluations of how others should act (and she can recognize that she is using a different behavior standard than they are). Some of her anger also emerged from a tendency to catastrophize the outcome of this delay in the moment.

I asked her to estimate how long the behavior of other parents delayed her on a typical morning. Her answer: less than five minutes most days. Frustrating for sure, but hardly catastrophic. She could see how minor it really was once she

---

* Feelings of guilt are useful too. Just as anger alerts us to having been wronged, guilt alerts us to having wronged someone else.

was away from it and not in the angering moment. In the end, evaluating the event this way meant that she refocused her energy and thoughts from "other people are behaving badly" to "this situation is frustrating but not catastrophic." Such a change may sound minor, but it is not. The former evaluation is largely hopeless – we cannot change the behavior of others. The latter evaluation offers some reason for optimism.

What does my anger tell me about me?

Evaluating our angering situations this way can reveal a lot about the circumstances we are in and what we might do to change them. Yet, when we dig deeper into these three elements, we realize there is a lot more there. The patterns we might see across situations reveal a lot about who we are at our core. Our anger is telling us something, not just about the specific situation, but about ourselves, who we are, and what we care about.

Let us start with the easier part to evaluate: the pre-anger state. It is important for people to look for trends in the relationship between their anger and their other feeling states (such as fatigue, hunger, stress). When you look back at the last few times you have been angry, and you think about your pre-anger state, are there particular conditions or moods that stand out as common? Perhaps you recognize that you tend to snap when you are under stress or are otherwise anxious. Maybe you recognize that you get most angry when you are tired. Identifying these elements of what triggers your anger is helpful in two ways. First, it offers a solution with regard to preventing unwanted anger. We will talk more about this in the next chapter, but if you notice that you get angry when you are hungry, try not to let yourself get so hungry. Second, even when you cannot prevent those triggering states, paying attention to them in the moment can help you cope with unwanted anger. In other words, saying to yourself "This all feels worse because I am tired" can go a long way to helping you cope.

Some of this may seem obvious; of course being hungry or tired makes us more likely to anger. Of course it makes those very real provocations feel even worse. But not everyone realizes this, and not everyone realizes it in the moment. Take for example the classic 1983 study by Drs. Norbert Schwarz and Gerald Clore[47] where 93 participants were asked via a telephone survey "How satisfied or dissatisfied are you with your life as a whole these days?" and participants answered on a scale of one to ten with ten being most satisfied.

Now, the researchers kept track of the weather for the locations they called, and they found that people reported a lower level of life satisfaction when it was raining than they did on a sunny day. While that may not sound surprising (weather does influence mood after all), keep in mind that they are asking, not about how they are feeling right then, but their overall life satisfaction. That is different and the current weather should not influence how satisfied we are with our life overall. The weather at this particular moment, while relevant to my current mood, should be largely irrelevant to how satisfied I am with my life overall. What seemed to be happening was that weather influenced current mood, and current mood influenced overall life satisfaction.

Here is the particularly interesting part, though. When the researcher drew attention to the weather in a second group of participants by asking "By the way, how's the weather down there?" the effect went away. People no longer reported a lower level of satisfaction with their life. By paying attention to the irrelevant thing, they stopped letting it influence them in the same way. Though this study is on a different subject than hunger or sleep deprivation and anger, I would argue that the same thing happens here. If we acknowledge the irrelevant thing that is influencing our mood, its influence over us will decrease.

Moving away from the pre-anger state and to the stimulus and appraisal, I wrote in chapter 2 about a few different situations that often lead to anger: injustice, poor-treatment, and goal-blocking. While anything can be a precipitant, including memories or even imagined events, individuals often have specific situations, people, and actions that tend to anger them most. We can learn a lot about ourselves by asking why specific things anger us. What is it about how *we* are appraising this particular person, situation, or behavior that leads to anger?

For example, imagine that you are someone who tends to get angry over other people's lateness. You recognize this recurring pattern about yourself, so the next step is to ask yourself *why* this is such a provocation for you. Why is your interpretation of this behavior of others leading you to anger? When I have asked people this question – why are they bothered by lateness – they say things like the following:

- It's disrespectful.
- It's like they think their time is more important than mine.
- I'm busy, and I don't like waiting around for people when I could be doing things.
- I have to be on time, so why don't they?

For the record, I think all of these interpretations are fairly reasonable. They may be incomplete in that punctuality problems are often driven by organizational and planning deficits as much as anything else, but they still seem like mostly reasonable interpretations. However, there are two very different issues underlying these appraisals and each of them says something different about what matters to the appraiser. Some of these speak to feelings of unjust or demeaning treatment. When someone says "It's disrespectful," or "They think their time is more important than mine," or "I have to be on time so why don't they?" what they are voicing is that they feel they are being treated unfairly or degraded in some way. This interpretation speaks to issues of ego and esteem.

On the other hand, when someone says "I'm busy, and I don't like waiting around for people" they are voicing a very different concern. This is an issue of having their goals blocked. They want to accomplish things and this late person is interfering with their ability to do so. Same scenario as above, same behavior from the other person, same emotion, but a different appraisal that is driven by a different core value.

This is important because particular personality styles are related to the experience and expression of anger. We covered one of those earlier – Type A personality – when we discussed the physical health consequences of anger. There are plenty of others, though, and one of the best places to start with such discussions is the "Big Five." If you are not familiar with the Big Five personality traits, these are five personality traits that were identified by Drs. Paul Costa and Robert McCrae: openness, conscientiousness, extraversion, agreeableness, and neuroticism.*

Research on the Big Five and anger has consistently found relationships between neuroticism, agreeableness, extraversion, and anger. In the 2017 study mentioned earlier, for example, Garcia-Sancho and colleagues had also included a personality questionnaire and found that neuroticism and agreeableness were highly related to anger. In the case of agreeableness, it is negatively correlated so if you are not agreeable, you are likely to experience chronic anger. A few years earlier in 2015, Drs. Christopher Pease and Gary Lewis explored this link and found a similar pattern.

What you can do when you evaluate these situations, is think about what your angry reaction might tell you about your personality. Did your reaction, for example, reflect a

---

* These can be remembered using the acronyms "OCEAN" or "CANOE." I, however, am not a great speller so often have to use the Big Five personality traits as my mnemonic device to remember how to spell "canoe."

tendency to be moody, nervous, or to worry (neuroticism)? Did it reflect an unwillingness to be kind, sympathetic, or helpful (agreeableness)? In the example above, one of those interpretations – "I'm busy, and I don't like waiting around" – might reflect more of a Type A personality style whereas the others likely reflect more of an absence of agreeableness.

To provide one more example, imagine you are scrolling through your favorite social media site and you see someone posting political opinions that are vastly different from yours. This is a common source of anger for people, but few stop to think about why they get angry over this. We all know that there are many people with different political opinions from us, so why does witnessing them make us angry? For some, it is an issue of goal-blocking. They want to live in a particular type of community surrounded by people who care about issues in the same way they do. When they come across people who feel differently, they interpret it as a barrier to their goal. They think, "We'll never make progress on [issue] if people like this exist," and they become angry.

I spoke to a friend about this once, though, and she said something different. "It makes me think that they think I'm dumb," she told me.

"Why?" I asked.

"Because I think they're dumb," she laughed in response.

But then she explained that she feels like the issues are so obvious and that she cannot figure out how they do not see that. She said she ends up feeling hurt because they do not seem to value her opinion or her perspective. When she makes what she thinks is a good argument and they do not change their mind, she feels like they must think she is stupid. She wants them to understand her position and why she thinks the way she does. Ultimately, she wants to win the argument and have them come around to her side. When they do not, she feels hurt and angry. "I'm right," she said, "and it kills me that they don't see that." For her, it is partly an issue of goal-blocking, but it is even more an issue of self-worth.

In both these examples, there is nothing inherently wrong with the anger response. Anger may be a completely reasonable response to these provocations. What is more interesting here is unpacking where that anger comes from in these situations. Once you develop a better sense of those patterns of thoughts, you start to better understand yourself and what is important to you.

ACTIVITY: DRILLING DOWN TO CORE BELIEFS

Here is a four-step process to better understand the core values and beliefs you hold that drive your anger.

I   Identify a few different *types* of situations where you tend to become angry. Though the goal is to identify types of situations, it might be helpful to come up with some specific examples of times when you became angry and then ask yourself if there is a pattern or tendency here. For example, I might say, "I got angry just now because my kids were arguing instead of playing in their rooms like I told them too."* Then, I would ask if this was a relatively consistent pattern.†

2   Identify the appraisals or interpretations that are most relevant across these situations. It may be helpful to start with the five types of appraisals discussed throughout the book: catastrophic evaluating, inflammatory labeling, demandingness, misattributing causation, and overgeneralizing. However, there may be others too.

---

* This did indeed just happen.

† It is, yes.

3   Try to drill down deeper to ask yourself what this appraisal tendency says about you and your personality. For example, if you find that you tend to catastrophize, does that reflect a more pessimistic or neurotic personality? If you see yourself often labeling people negatively, does that reflect a more general attitude of contempt?

4   Make a plan, moving forward, to consider this when you diagram angry incidents in the future. Be prepared to ask yourself, "Is my tendency to be pessimistic driving this anger right now?" or "Is the result of my tendency to be closed minded?"

One piece of a bigger puzzle

Of course, understanding our anger and ourselves, while an important part of the process, is but one piece of a bigger puzzle. To have a healthy relationship with our anger, we have to know how to manage it. We have to put personal practices in place (habits, behaviors, thoughts) that allow us to cope with anger in both the immediate and the long term.

CHAPTER 11

MANAGING ANGER

Public service announcement

When I was a kid, there was a public service announcement that would come on during Saturday morning cartoons that went something like "When you feel yourself getting tense, stop ... two ... three .... breathe ... two ... three. Think your way to sense." It may sound incredibly trite, but it must have worked because here I am 35 years later, and I still remember it. I bring it up because this is what anger management looks like to most people. When you find yourself getting angry, you try and stay in control and work your way out of it through deep breathing. There is nothing wrong with this at all other than that it is incomplete. Anger management does include deep breathing when you are angry, but it can also include so much more than that.

In chapter 2, we talked about diagraming our angry incidents to better understand our anger and ourselves. There is another reason to engage in this practice, though, and it is because once we know why we became angry, we can intervene at any place in that model to deal with our anger more effectively. That may include relaxation through deep breathing or visualization, but it could also include a number of other practices. Some of those practices include things you can do in the moment, but some of them are bigger-picture ways you can restructure your day-to-day activities to feel less unwanted anger.

Imagine the following

Let us imagine the following hypothetical example. You are driving to work and have a really big day ahead of you. You have quite a few important meetings, some of which you need some additional time to prepare for when you get to the office. You wanted to get to the office a little earlier, so you skipped breakfast. It feels like there is a little more traffic than usual, and you are starting to get agitated. You also start to feel like you are getting stopped at more red lights than usual, and the commute is taking longer than expected. You are starting to become even more frustrated because you tried to do all the right things. You had a big day so you left early for work to get ahead of some things, and now you are going to get there at the same time you would have had you left when you usually do. "I could have had breakfast," you think to yourself. "Instead, I'm starving, *and* I'm going to be behind in my work."

As you get closer to the office, you get stuck behind another driver who obviously does not know where they are going. They are quite slow, and each time they get to a street they slow down, probably to look at the street sign and see if this is where they should turn. "What is this idiot doing?" you ask. You cannot pass them safely, so you feel trapped behind them. You flash your lights and honk to let them know that they are slowing you down, but you cannot tell if they even notice. Now, you are not just going to get there at the normal time, you are going to be late. You become irate as you think about work. "Today is going to suck" you say to yourself. "I have so much to do and I'm not going to get to any of it. God, why does stuff like this always happen to me?"

Diagraming the incident

Now, let us walk through each part of this incident with the model we have been using, starting with the precipitant: being slowed down on the way to work. This is a classic example of goal-blocking. You have a specific goal in mind, to get to work a little early, and it is being thwarted. Interestingly, it is not just one person or event that is blocking your goal, but a combination of things (traffic, red lights, another driver). Of course, this is happening within the context of two different anger-provoking feeling states (pre-anger states): hunger and stress. You have a big day ahead of you that you are feeling nervous about, and you skipped breakfast to give yourself time to get to prepare – which seems to have backfired.

When it comes to appraisal, we can identify a couple of different types of thoughts here including some catastrophizing ("Today is going to suck"), inflammatory labeling ("What is this idiot doing?"), and overgeneralizing ("Why does stuff like this *always* happen to me?"). You can also see some assumptions in there about how the day is going to go ("I'm going to be behind in my work" and "I have so much to do and I'm not going to get to any of it"). Those predictions may end up being accurate, but they may not, and you are becoming angry in response to those predictions before they even happen. Taken together, while this situation might be frustrating for anyone, regardless of pre-anger state or appraisal, there are subtle interpretations in this instance that magnify that anger.

Managing pre-anger states

I have mentioned this in previous chapters, but there are ways of managing our pre-anger states that can help us minimize unwanted anger. If we think through some of the states most likely to exacerbate anger, we come up with a list like the following:

1 Stressed or worried
2 Running late
3 Hungry

4 Sleepy
5 Physically uncomfortable

Although it can be difficult sometimes, it is far from impossible to mitigate these different states. While not everyone has this privilege, many of us can make sure we do not get to a place where we are hungry or are running late. We can take steps to deal with unwanted stress or anxiety that might make us prone to anger. We can take steps to improve our sleep so that we do not find ourselves cranky because of our fatigue.

In the example above, imagine how the situation might have been different had you taken another approach to the day. Perhaps knowing you had a busy work day ahead, you went to bed earlier, woke up earlier, and had a healthy breakfast. You might be dealing with the exact same situation externally (same precipitant), but your mood going into it would likely have changed if you were well fed and rested. Note that having had breakfast would have subtly changed your appraisal as well. Instead of "I'm starving and I'm going to be behind in my work" it is just "I'm going to be behind in my work." It may sound small but if we think of anger as sometimes being the results of a bunch of little things adding up, removing some of those little things will help.

Managing provocations

A friend of mine used to read and respond to comments at the bottom of online news articles in his local paper. He would sometimes spend hours arguing with strangers about politics, getting angry while doing it. Later, he would call me and vent about things people had written to him or just posted in response. He would get fired up all over again as he discussed it with me. At one point I asked him, "Why do you read those if they make you so mad?"

He laughed and said: "I don't know. I tell myself I'm trying to change people's minds but I know that doesn't really work."

So to be clear, I am not suggesting that he or anyone should always avoid conversations that make them angry or otherwise uncomfortable. Far from it. This example is simply to illustrate that we make choices about who we interact with and how we interact with them. Those choices influence the feelings we have. To some degree, we can choose what provocations we experience. If reading political comments from strangers makes us mad and we do not want to feel mad, we can choose not to do it.

If we compare this with another feeling state like fear, it becomes much easier to realize how odd it is that we voluntarily expose ourselves to things that make us angry. About ten years ago, I decided that even though I enjoyed scary movies in the moment, I did not like how they made me feel afterwards. I had experienced too many sleepless nights as a consequence of watching scary movies and decided they were not good for me. So I stopped watching them for the most part. The caveat here is that if a scary movie comes out that I have heard is really good or really important (such as *Get Out* or *The Invisible Man*), I will make a point of seeing it. I have decided that, in some cases, it is worth feeling scared in order to see a really important and well-made movie.

Dr. James Gross described this as "situation selection" in his 2002 article on emotion regulation.[48] Situation selection is "approaching or avoiding certain people, places, or things so as to regulate emotion." He uses the example of choosing to go to a friend's house instead of a study session the night before a big exam. The person is selecting an activity that makes them happy instead of one that makes them anxious. In the case of anger, imagine you have a colleague who rubs you the wrong way. This person frequently says and does things that you become angry about. Now, this person has a work party that you are invited to. You can decide whether or not you go to that party. If you identify it as a potential provocation, you have the choice over whether you participate.

But what if the party is something you sort of have to go to? What if it would harm your career to not go or if your absence would be a little too obvious to your boss or other coworkers? You can also change how you interact with situations like these (what Gross called "situation modification"). You can bring a friend or partner to the event to serve as buffer between you and your irritating coworker. You can tell a trusted colleague how you are feeling and ask them to "save you" in those instances where you are talking with the irritating coworker one-on-one.

In the example earlier, where you are late to work on an important day, it is a little harder to identify how you could have avoided this trigger. Some provocations just come up and are unavoidable. However, even in those relatively unexpected situations like traffic, we can find ways to avoid these triggers. One client I worked with rearranged her work schedule to stay a little later every day so she would not leave at the busiest time of day. Another started to take a different route to work. He said it took about the same amount of time because, though it was a greater distance, there was less traffic – it was a more peaceful drive and therefore worth it.

It is fair to ask if this sort of "cue avoidance" is healthy. Is it good for us to avoid the things that make us angry? In the context of a similar emotion like fear, for example, avoidance is what drives the development of quite a few disorders like phobias and obsessive-compulsive disorder and exacerbates other disorders like post-traumatic stress disorder. Might it not also have a similar effect for anger? Would it not be better to learn to cope with those things that anger us instead of avoiding them?

The answer to these questions is more complicated than I would like it to be. Avoidance is one of the trickier types of behaviors when it comes to anger. Dr. Eric Dahlen and I did a study on this back in 2007 when we gave people a variety of questionnaires associated with anger.[49] One of them was the Behavioral Anger Response Questionnaire (BARQ)[50] which was developed by a team of researchers to measure six different anger expression styles. One of those was avoidance, which includes attempts to forget the angering event or finding ways to distract yourself from the angering event.

We found that avoidance negatively correlated with one's tendency to get angry, so the more people actively tried to avoid angering events or memories, the less anger they tended to feel. Avoidance was also correlated with healthy expression styles like deep breathing, seeking social support, and working through anger by listening to music or writing poetry. At the same time, though, it was correlated with anger suppression, which is known to be a negative expression style and correlated with a variety of health and interpersonal consequences, such as cardiovascular disorders and alienating friends, family, and coworkers. We have likely all had a friend who would say "It's fine" when we know it is not *really* fine. Such attempts at suppression can be irritating to people.

In this study, avoidance was essentially both good and bad depending on the variable we compared it with. Though it is impossible to know for sure, this likely speaks to the complicated and contextual nature of avoidance. It is both good and bad depending on the very specific context of the situation you are in and what you are avoiding. How do you know if this is the good type of avoidance or the bad type of avoidance? Arguably, by weighing out both the short-term and long-term benefits and consequences.

Revisiting the example from my friend who would argue with others online for hours, let us consider what the short-term and long-term consequences might be to avoiding this behavior. Honestly, in this case it does not feel like there are any realistic consequences, short-term or long-term, to stopping. I suppose you could argue that it might be good for him to learn to disagree with people without getting angry, but that feels like a stretch. On some of these disagreements, it made perfect sense for him to be angry. This is really more of a question of whether he needed to invite those disagreements into his life as often as he was.

Looking at the driving example we started with, though, makes things a little more complicated. Ultimately, traffic is something we are likely to encounter regularly and there are a variety of similar experiences we encounter as well like long lines and other sorts of delays and goal-blocking. It might be better for you to learn to cope with that frequent life experience rather than avoid it each day. Perhaps the healthiest approach is to avoid it on those days when we do not feel we have the emotional capacity to deal with it, but to make an effort to embrace it on those days we feel we want to learn to cope with frustration. Like exercise, there are days when we want to exert ourselves fully and other days when we need to rest.

Managing appraisals

The bulk of the work we do to manage our anger happens in the third part of the "Why we get mad" model that was discussed in chapter 2: cognitive appraisal. How we interpret the stimulus is ultimately the most important part of why we get angry in a given situation. In the example above, we saw catastrophizing, inflammatory labeling, overgeneralizing, and others. But what if the appraisal had been different? What if you had simply said to yourself, "This is frustrating on such an important day, but I can deal with it"? What if you spent that time in the car thinking about how you can solve the problems caused by the delay without catastrophizing? Though it is difficult to identify them at the time, there are infinite interpretations of an event and many of them will not lead to anger.

Here is a quick reminder of the five types of thoughts most associated with anger:

- **Overgeneralizing:** Describing events in overly broad ways ("This *always* happens to me").
- **Demandingness:** Expecting others to put their needs aside in favor of our needs ("That person should stop what they are doing to come and help me").

- **Misattributing causation:** Assigning blame or interpreting causation incorrectly ("They did that on purpose just to annoy me").
- **Catastrophizing:** Blowing things out of proportion ("This is going to ruin my entire day").
- **Inflammatory labeling:** Labeling people or situations in highly negative ways ("That guy is a total idiot").

There are, of course, others that will be relevant at times. Self-blame, for example, may be relevant in times of anger at oneself. We may read other people's minds ("He must think I'm a fool") or personalize events ("Why is this happening to me?") in ways that lead to anger. These five, though, are the biggies. These are the thoughts people tend to gravitate to when they get angry.

There are two important steps to managing these thoughts. First, we have to identify them in the moment. Second, we have to consider some alternatives. To be honest, learning to identify them in the moment is probably the most difficult part for people. It takes effort not just when they are angry, but when they are not angry. They have to be willing to think about their thoughts in the moment of anger and outside of that moment when they reflect back on it.

There are a few different ways of doing this. One is to evaluate past angering events. Right now, think back to a time you were very angry and answer the following questions about it.

1 What was the stimulus?
2 On a scale of one to ten, how angry were you?
3 What thoughts did you have at the time? List all of them that you can remember. Try and think through without considering what type of thought it was or even whether it was incorrect. Just list them nonjudgmentally.

When you have done this, consider each of those thoughts individually. In retrospect, were they accurate and realistic interpretations of the situation? Were any of them consistent with the five types of thoughts I have described? To what degree did you question your ability to cope with the situation?

A more formal way of doing this is using a mood log. A mood log is just as it sounds – a log of emotional situations where you keep track of different thoughts, feelings, and behaviors you had at the time. It is a strategy therapists often use to help mood-disordered clients become aware of the relationship between their thoughts and feelings, but there is no reason a mood log can only be used in cases of diagnosable mental-health problems. They can be used by anyone who wants to have a healthier emotional life.

Mood logs can also include whatever variables you want to keep track of. Some mood logs might include a place for alternative thoughts or a place for behaviors that followed the feeling. It really depends on the goal. For now, let us use a mood log with just five columns: situation, emotion, intensity, primary appraisal (thoughts about the precipitant or stimulus), and secondary appraisal (thoughts about your ability to cope with the situation). I have filled one line with the example from above.

Situation	Emotion(s)	Intensity (scale of 1 to 10)	Primary appraisal	Secondary appraisal
Late to work due to unexpected traffic.	Anger, but also some worry.	Anger: 8 Worry: 7	What is this idiot doing? Why does this stuff always happen to me?	Today is going to suck. I have so much to do and now I'm not going to get to any of it.

Again, one of the really great things about mood logs like this is that you can adapt them to what you believe is important for you. If you want to focus more on your pre-anger state, for example, you can add a column where you keep track of that. If you want to explore what this anger might be telling you about

your personality, you could add a column where you reflect on the
traits that might be driving your response (such as impatience or
closed mindedness). Mood logs are a great tool for helping people
better understand their feelings and manage them.

One column that is often included in a mood log is a space
for some alternative thoughts. For those times when you
determine that the thoughts you had were unreasonable or
unrealistic and exacerbated your anger (remember, sometimes
there is nothing unreasonable or unrealistic about your anger
at all), the next step is to explore some more reasonable
alternatives. Above, for example, perhaps some alternative
thoughts could be "This is frustrating for sure, and I don't like it
when things like this happen to me" or "This is going to make
me ten minutes later than I had hoped. I'll have to adjust."

The value of both of these statements is that they are
accurate and realistic. They are not dishonest interpretations
that minimize the real consequences of the situation. You
are not saying "Everything will be fine" because they might
not be fine. You are not saying "It's no big deal" because it
might be a big deal. You are embracing a truthful and sensible
understanding of the situation you found yourself in and that
interpretation leads to a slightly different emotional outcome.

There are a variety of alternative appraisals people engage in
when faced with seemingly negative events that might lead to
a healthier emotional outcome. In 2001, three psychologists
developed the Cognitive Emotion Regulation Questionnaire
(CERQ)[51] to measure different types of thoughts people
have when they experience a negative event. Some of these
we have already discussed. Like a lot of thought surveys, the
CERQ measures self-blame, other-blame, rumination, and
catastrophizing. What makes this survey interesting, though, is
that it also measures some thoughts that are typically associated
with more positive emotional experiences. Specifically, refocus
on planning, positive refocus, positive reappraisal, acceptance,
and putting into perspective.

Refocusing on planning is when we think about what we need to do to solve the problem we are facing or handle this situation we are in. Positive refocus is when we try to think about more positive experiences we have had in the past. So, we are essentially taking ourselves away from the situation and focusing on other less-upsetting experiences. Positive reappraisal is when we try to reinterpret the same event in a more positive light. Acceptance is attempting to tolerate the situation as something we cannot change. Finally, when we put things into perspective, we are thinking of the event in terms of its broader significance by minimizing how catastrophic it might actually be compared with other negative experiences.

In 2005, we did a study where we investigated the CERQ as it relates to anger.[52] We had nearly 400 participants take the CERQ along with several measures of anger, stress, anxiety, and depression. We were trying to determine which of these nine thought types were most problematic and which were most adaptive in terms of minimizing anger. By and large, we found what you would expect. Blaming others, blaming yourself, catastrophizing, and rumination were all related to anger. People who engaged in these types of thoughts became angry more often and expressed that anger in unhealthy ways.

With the other thoughts that were regarded as more adaptive, though, things were a little more complicated. People who refocused on planning, thought about more positive things or tried to put things into perspective did not necessarily get angry less than others, but they did express their anger in healthier ways when they did get angry.* If you had to pick the best type of positive thought from this study, it would be positive reappraisal, when we try to reinterpret situations in a more positive way. This thought type led to less anger and healthier expression styles.

---

* They were also less likely to become depressed, anxious, or stressed, so the benefits of such positive thinking extend well beyond anger.

These alternative thoughts are about both primary and secondary appraisal. When you reappraise a negative situation in a positive light you are both changing your evaluation of the provocation and rethinking what it takes to cope with this negative event. This is important because secondary appraisal, or how well you think you can cope with a negative event, is critical to managing anger. In the example described earlier about driving to work, much of the anger was rooted in your perceived lack of ability to cope with the delay. When you say "Today is going to suck," what you are really saying is that you are powerless to fix it.

How can we shift an appraisal from a sense of helplessness to empowerment? This is where thought types like refocusing on planning are particularly valuable. When people shift from catastrophizing ("This is going to ruin my day") to planning ("This is frustrating, so how do I fix it?"), they stop thinking of themselves as a passive player in the situation and become someone who actually has the power to adjust to the circumstances.

ACTIVITY: RETHINKING ANGERING THOUGHTS

This activity is to help you rethink some of your angering thoughts in less angering but realistic ways. The goal is not for you to lie to yourself in order to feel less angry (it's not about shifting from "This is terrible" to "It's no big deal"). Instead, try to identify subtle shifts that might be more positive and empowering.

1   Make a list of thoughts you had from a time you were angry.
2   To the best of your ability, identify what type of thought it was (such as catastrophizing or inflammatory labeling).

3 Identify an accurate but less angering alternative thought. I have provided some examples below.

Angering thought	Thought type	Alternative thought
He always does this!	Overgeneralizing	He does this more than I would like.
This will ruin everything	Catastrophizing	This is bad, and we're going to have to strategize on how to fix it.
Why can't they just get this right!?	Misattributing causation, inflammatory labeling	This person continues to struggle with this and may need help working through it.

Beyond acceptance

There is one purportedly positive thought type that does not seem to make much of a difference with regard to anger. People are often told to accept the things they cannot change. Yet, attempts at acceptance were not only unrelated to anger, they were associated with depression and stress. When you try to simply accept a negative situation without changing it – when you say "I will simply tolerate this negative experience because there is nothing I can do about it" – not only does it have zero impact on anger, it leads to additional stress and sadness. This one finding suggests something very important about anger: that feeling it and doing nothing with it is not good for us. We need to find ways to use it for positive change.

CHAPTER 12
USING ANGER

Diagnosing anger

At this point, I have outlined a host of problems that can emerge from chronic or poorly controlled anger. From violence to problems of mental and physical health to relationship difficulties, anger can have catastrophic consequences to the lives of those who cannot control their anger as well as those around them. Yet, despite all of these potential problems, anger is not considered a mental-health issue in the same way as other maladaptive emotions. Whereas depression reflects maladaptive sadness and the anxiety disorders reflect maladaptive versions of fear, there is no such disorder for maladaptive anger listed in the most recent version of the *Diagnostic and Statistical Manual of Mental Disorders (DSM-5)*,* or any of the past versions for that matter.

Frankly, it is an odd omission that I cannot fully explain. The American Psychiatric Association has long been criticized for over-pathologizing relatively routine human experiences,

---

* Somehow, this big book of diagnosable mental-health conditions can list everything from "major depressive disorder, single episode with melancholic features and peripartum onset" to "sleep-related hypoventilation" to "conduct disorder, childhood onset with limited prosocial emotions." It does not, however, list any anger disorders.

so it feels particularly odd to see them potentially under-pathologizing in this case. It is not that they have ignored anger altogether. There are several places where anger or something similar like irritability is listed as a symptom of some other condition. For example, anger is described as a symptom of borderline personality disorder, post-traumatic stress disorder, and premenstrual dysphoric disorder.

What is particularly interesting, though, is how often anger is thought of as symptom of depression. Irritability is listed as a symptom of both major depressive disorder and persistent depressive disorder, and it is noted in the criteria that irritability is only a symptom in children and adolescents. A brand-new depressive disorder to the *DSM-5* that feels closest to an anger disorder is called disruptive mood dysregulation disorder (DMDD), which includes irritability, incidents of verbal abuse, and physical aggression. Again, though, DMDD is listed as a depressive disorder and can only be diagnosed if the first outburst occurs before the age of 18. It appears that the authors of the *DSM-5* believe that anger is primarily a symptom of depression in children.

Ultimately, anger should be thought of much like the other emotion-rooted disorders in the *DSM-5*. We recognize that sadness is healthy much of the time, but can become pathological when too severe or long lasting (as in major depressive disorder). We recognize that fear is healthy much of the time, but can become pathological when we become unreasonably afraid of particular objects or situations (such as specific phobias and social anxiety disorder). So why have we been so reluctant to consider anger a healthy emotion that can become pathological when long-lasting, severe, or poorly expressed?

The proposed disorders

Anger's relative absence from the *DSM-5* is not due to a lack of trying from anger researchers. There are at least four different anger-related disorders that have been written up as potential diagnostic criteria. The most interesting of these to me is anger regulation-expression disorder (ARED) because it was written as a replacement for something already in the *DSM-5*: intermittent explosive disorder (IED). IED, as mentioned in chapter 6, is an impulse-control disorder where people cannot resist the urge to strike out verbally or physically. While it is reasonable to assume that there is some anger behind these aggressive episodes, by now you know that even if we consider IED an anger disorder, it is still a very narrow view of how anger can be expressed. There is nothing in the IED diagnostic criteria that captures non-aggressive but still problematic expressions of anger.

Drs. DiGiuseppe and Tafrate[53] wrote up criteria for ARED that captures the symptoms of IED while also including other aspects of problematic anger that are not currently included in IED. For example, along with verbal and physical aggression, ARED includes more indirect or passive forms of aggression (such as sarcasm, covertly sabotaging, spreading rumors). The authors also recognized that anger need not lead to any particular type of external expression to be a problem for the person. The criteria include two categories of symptoms: angry affect and aggressive/expressive behaviors. The first category is for those recurring anger experiences that, though they are not aggressive, lead to a variety of negative consequence (rumination, ineffective communication, and withdrawal being examples). The second group of symptoms is for the aggressive or expressive behaviors associated with anger. This group includes the symptoms of IED (such as physical aggression) along with some forms of passive aggression (disrupting or negatively influencing others' social networks).* It is possible that someone could fit into both of these categories and so the criteria include three different subtypes based on which symptoms the person has.

I want to note that like almost every disorder in the *DSM-5*, you would only be diagnosed with this if "there is evidence of regular damage to social or vocational relationships due to the anger episodes or expressive patterns." In other words, you would not be diagnosed with this unless there was a clear and consistent pattern of problems resulting from your anger. Again, as with sadness and fear, the idea here is not to pathologize the experience of anger automatically, but to recognize that it *can* become a problem.

There are two things you will notice about the criteria. The first, it speaks to new parts of the "Why we get mad" model that we have not talked about as much yet: the feelings of anger (the actual feeling state) and anger expressions (how we express our anger when we are mad). This proposed diagnosis is largely reflective of the feelings of anger themselves and the expressions of those feelings. It has nothing to do with the provocations, pre-anger states, or appraisals.

The second, it acknowledges what I think is one of the most important things about anger: that how you express it matters a great deal. It is when we get into a pattern of maladaptive expression styles that anger becomes a problem. When we manage it and use it in a healthy way, it can be a powerful force in our lives. So, how do we do that? There are a quite a few ways.

---

* The criteria for ARED are proof that scientists can make anything sound more complicated via jargon. Spreading rumors becomes "negatively influencing others' social networks," foul language becomes "aversive verbalizations," and giving someone the finger becomes "negative gesticulation" (which is a specific type of "provocative bodily expression").

Think of anger as fuel

In chapter 3, we talked about how your amygdala kicks off a cascade of physiological responses when you become angry. Adrenaline floods your body, your heart rate increases, your muscles tense up, and your breathing increases as your body prepares for a fight. You can think of your anger as fuel. It literally provides you with the energy and power necessary to change things that need changing and solve problems that need solving. Sometimes those problems are small. You have had a leaky faucet for months and one day, for some combination of reasons (precipitant, pre-anger state, appraisal), it frustrates you to the point that you drop everything and fix it.

Sometimes those problems are massive, though. You witness an injustice so egregious that you simply cannot stand it. A situation that is truly and objectively catastrophic. You read an article about climate destruction, see a video of police brutality, learn a new fact about the frequency of sexual harassment or online bullying, and you become livid with the state of things. Your anger kicks in and fuels your desire to do something. You donate to an organization, attend a protest, write a letter to your local paper, or do something even more significant. That rage you felt provided the spark you needed to commit yourself to making a difference. It both tells you something is wrong and energizes you to right that wrong.

Like any fuel, though, there are caveats. First, just as fuel is volatile, so is anger. There is the very real possibility of an unwanted explosion when you are not careful enough. Second, that fuel will eventually burn up, leaving your tank empty if you do not refill. There are strategies for combating both of these potential problems.

Keep your anger in check

Even when we are right to be angry, we may need to find ways of keeping that anger in check so we do not explode. In the last chapter, we talked about managing anger through managing provocations, states, and interpretations. But what if our interpretations are right? How do we manage our anger when someone truly is to blame, when we are not asking for special treatment but fair treatment, or when the situation truly is catastrophic?

Again, you only need to keep your anger in check if you think you might do something irresponsible as a result of it. As I talked about earlier, there are times when anger interferes in our ability to think clearly. We may solve the problems more effectively if we have calmed down. One of the best approaches to dealing with unwanted angry feelings is through relaxation. It works the same way for anger as it would with an anxiety problem. Anger and relaxation are what we call incompatible mood states meaning you cannot feel them at the same time. Just as you cannot be relaxed and scared at the same time, you cannot be relaxed and angry at the same time.

There are a variety of relaxation approaches people can use when they feel angry and they mostly involve some sort of deep breathing and/or distraction. On the deep-breathing side, we see everything from the quick "triangle breathing" approach (breath in for three seconds, hold for three seconds, breath out for three seconds) to the longer approach of finding a comfortable spot away from people and going through some short deep-breathing exercises. In many ways, it depends on what you might need (how angry are you?) and what you can do at the time (are you able to get away?). For example, there are times when the anger is mild enough that even though you feel the need to keep it in check, a quick moment of putting your head back, taking a deep breath, and releasing it is enough to help you focus again. There are other times, though, where getting away from people and finding a quiet spot for five to ten minutes for a deep breathing exercise might be necessary.

An additional variation on deep breathing might include progressive muscle relaxation where you target specific muscle groups with tension and relaxation. Take a moment right now, for example, and make a tight fist, hold it for three seconds, and let it go. What you might notice is a strong sense of relaxation fills your hand and fingers as you relaxed. One of my college psychology professors likened this to a pendulum swinging back and forth, from tension to relaxation, a metaphor that sat nicely with me. The procedure for progressive muscle relaxation can vary, but people typically will start by lying down, taking a few deep breaths, and then tensing the muscles in their feet for three to five seconds before relaxing for three to five seconds. They then move up to their calves, thighs, and throughout the rest of their body including their forehead and jaw.

On the distraction side of things, people will often integrate guided visualizations into their deep breathing. Visualization is when people use some sort of mental imagery to take themselves away from the angering situation into a place that is more relaxing. They may envision a particular setting or activity they find soothing (often places in nature like the beach or a forest).* For some this might mean lying down at the beach, soaking up some sun, while listening to imaginary waves crashing on the shore. For others, it might mean taking a long walk through the forest. The specifics might come down to what people are best at. If you have a good imagination, you might be able to take yourself away to any place whether you have been there before or not. Others might need to imagine a place they have been before or even a specific day when they found themselves particularly relaxed. Still others may embrace some sort of guided visualization via audio recording where a narrator takes them through a relaxing scenario.

---

* The research on nature and relaxation is particularly fascinating. Related to the evolutionary perspectives on emotion, there are many scholars who suggest that our evolutionary history primed us to feel restored by nature.

Refill on your own terms

The other side of the anger-as-fuel metaphor is that we sometimes run out of fuel when we need it most. Think about this in terms of broad societal problems or concerns you may have (such as environmental destruction, corruption, racism, sexism). Because we hear about these issues day in day out, it can be hard to maintain a meaningful level of anger. The popular culture term for this is "outrage fatigue." People feel a sense of exhaustion surrounding issues they care about because they are inundated with information about how bad things are. Outrage fatigue can lead to a sense of hopelessness ("It will never get better") and exhaustion ("I can't keep doing this"), which can be damaging to people. I often hear about people who choose to turn away from any form of civic engagement, including even following the news, because they just feel too sad or angry.

At the same time, outrage fatigue can include what psychologists refer to as "habituation." Habituation is when we get used to a stimulus in a way that it does not have as intense a response as it once did. Imagine there is construction outside of your office for a few days. At first, the sound of hammering might be annoying to you, but after a few days you get used to it. You have become habituated to that stimulus and no longer notice it. In terms of outrage fatigue, let us imagine you care deeply about the environment and support polices that protect it. The first time you hear about a particularly egregious policy from a president, governor, or other leader that will lead to environmental harm, you might become livid. Over time, though, as that person continues to pass such laws, you might become used to it (habituated) and consequently fail to become as angry as before.

From a "using anger" perspective, outrage fatigue is a problem. When we become habituated to the issues we face, whether they be personal frustrations like poor treatment at work or broader societal injustices, we lose the fuel necessary to make changes. Fatigued is the opposite of energized, so we need to find a way to maintain the energy that anger should provide us.

There are two ways to refill our anger fuel tank (both of which should be used cautiously given the negative consequences anger can often bring). First, when you are most angry about a problem, take a moment to reflect on how you are feeling. Remember that rage, so that you might be able to pull it up on your own later. Think about the provocation and pay attention to the thoughts you are having. Think about what you want to do with that anger. In some ways, this is the opposite of the visualization we talked about using to help you relax. This is visualization to help you stay angry at times when you really need it.

The second way of finding your anger is by actively seeking out those provocations. This is, essentially, the opposite of cue avoidance which we talked about in the last chapter. In the age of social media, it has never been easier to approach our anger cues. If you want to make yourself angry about politics, just go to your politically polar-opposite cousin's Facebook page and read some of their posts. Go to Twitter and figure out what is trending that you find infuriating.

This idea that we want to make ourselves angry might seem far-fetched to some, but if you consider it within the context of sports, it is actually quite commonplace. A student of mine, Kayla Hucke, did her senior honors project on this very concept with college-level athletes, exploring how they used anger and anxiety in their sports.[54] She had a sample of 169 student athletes and asked them how they wanted to feel on the day of, immediately before, and during a sporting event. She also assessed their emotional intelligence (their ability to understand, perceive, manage, and use emotions) and asked about times their anger and anxiety helped or hurt them in a sporting event.

The results were striking. Athletes wanted to start the day of a sporting event with a little bit of anger and they wanted to become even more angry as the day went on with the most anger they felt during the actual event. Contrast that with fear, where what they wanted was to be able to start the day anxious, feel a lot of anxiety right before the event, and have that anxiety dissipate while they were playing. While she found that anger during sports did have some perceived negative consequences (some athletes found it to be distracting or that their negativity might bring them or their teammates down), athletes also identified some real benefits to being angry when they competed. Specifically, their anger got their adrenaline pumping, increased their effort, and got them feeling more motivated. In other words, their anger *fueled* their performance. Finally, those athletes who scored highest on emotional intelligence were more successful in their sports performances. The people who could muster up that fuel on their own and channel it into their activities performed best.

Play through those ruminative thoughts

Have you ever found yourself after an angering situation unable to let it go? Maybe you find yourself playing the situation over and over in your mind, thinking about what you wish you had said? Or maybe it is a situation that has not actually happened yet, but you find yourself running through how you expect it to go and the different permutations of what you anticipate saying and being said to you? If so, you are not alone. This is a well-known emotion-related concept called rumination and it can be quite disconcerting for people.*

---

* I am going to use this time to confess that I am the very definition of a ruminator. In fact, when my son was three years old and I was driving home from daycare with him one time, I was having all sorts of ruminative, angry thoughts about my work day. We were listening to music and all of a sudden he said, "What did you say?" "I didn't say anything, buddy," I responded, to which he answered "Yeah, you did. You said, [repeated the entirety of my supposedly internal monolog]." This was the day I realized that either he could read minds ... or I do not just ruminate, I also talk to myself.

Earlier in the book, I mentioned a few studies we did, one using the Behavioral Anger Response Questionnaire (BARQ) and one using the Cognitive Emotion Regulation Questionnaire (CERQ). Both of these questionnaires have a subscale that measures rumination where they ask questions about brooding or continuing to think about the angering event. In the studies I have done using these questionnaires, we find a consistent pattern. Rumination is correlated with both the tendency to become angry and the maladaptive expression of anger (including the tendency to have vengeful thoughts and thoughts of violence). Interestingly, though, in both studies, rumination was most related to anger suppression. This means that if you tend to try and hold your anger in when you feel provoked, you are more likely to ruminate later.

If we think through the pattern here, it looks like this: People feel provoked, try not to respond to the provocation, but then cannot seem to stop thinking about it. In our 2004 study on this, we looked not just at anger but also depression, anxiety, and stress. Rumination was correlated with all three of these mood states as well. Now, there are a variety of ways to deal with unwanted rumination. In many ways, rumination comes from a similar place as worry, so, as with worry, one of the productive ways of dealing with it is distraction. You can read a book, listen to music, watch a movie or a TV show, or some other mechanism that will occupy your mind.

It would be easy to suggest that rumination is bad for you based on these and other findings. After all, it is correlated with anger, depression, anxiety, and stress, but there is another way of thinking about this pattern. Perhaps rumination is your mind's way of letting you know that you have not resolved the situation yet. The fact that your brain will not let it go probably means that you are not comfortable with the resolution. In short, rumination might be another way that your anger communicates to you that you or others you care about have been treated unjustly.

It is sort of like getting a song stuck in your head. When that happens, one of the ways to get rid of it is to sing it to completion – to get closure. With rumination, one of the ways to deal with it might be to try and get closure. Especially if you are ruminating *because* you suppressed your anger in the first place. It might be helpful to revisit the tough conversation where you suppressed your anger and this time assert yourself in a more direct way. Contact the person you are angry with and restart the conversation by saying something like, "The other day when [angering thing happened], I felt angry and didn't say anything." You may still not get the outcome you want from this new conversation (we cannot control how others respond to us), but you will likely feel more comfortable with how you handled your side of things.

Anger communication

One of the benefits of anger from an evolutionary perspective is that it aids in communication. As we discussed in chapter 3, all emotions are communication tools. The facial expressions we make when we are sad, scared, or angry convey something important to those around us. Our tears tell people that we need help. Our wide-open eyes and screams tell others that we are in danger (and, therefore, they might be in danger too). Our glares and frowns communicate that they may have wronged us and that our relationships need repairing.

We have obviously evolved past a place where we rely exclusively on our facial expressions and other nonverbals to convey emotion (though, our nonverbals are certainly still relevant). However, communicating our anger is still a valuable tool when it comes to using anger. This is especially true in those moments when our anger is justified. We have been wronged, we need to be able to communicate to the people who wronged us how we are feeling and why we are feeling that way. It can be difficult, but it is the first step to obtaining the resolution we might be looking for. Here are some tips for making the most of those difficult conversations.

Plan ahead for difficult conversations Think about what you points you want to make, how you are going to convey them, and how the other person may react (how will they likely feel and what might they say in response). You will not be able to plan for everything, but having a sense for what you want to convey ahead of time will help you get your point across and help you stay calm in the moment.

Practice "When this happened, I felt" statements Try to avoid statements like, "It *made* me mad when you …". Instead try, "When you …, I felt angry." It communicates essentially the same thing, but takes the onus off the other person. It is a way of acknowledging that you play a role in your own anger (without taking full responsibility either).

Maintain professionalism The last thing in the world I want to be in is the "tone police." I have already said that there is no one way to communicate anger and that sometimes yelling and screaming is the only way to be heard. That said, in these difficult conversations, trying to stay calm and professional can keep the other person from becoming defensive. Try not to call them names or yell. You will likely end up making more progress if you err on the side of assertiveness rather than aggressiveness.

Stay on topic Disagreements can easily get out of hand and get to a place where instead of resolving the dispute, you are just trying to score points. Try to keep the specific issue at the forefront of the conversation. If the point of the discussion is that you want your friend, for example, to know that you are angry because they lied to you, do not bring up all the other bad things they have done in your friendship. Keep it about the specific thing you are upset about.

Make sure to listen too Half of having difficult conversations is listening to what the other person has to say. Too often, instead of listening when the other person is talking, people spend that time thinking of what they want to say next. Try not to do that. Listen and pay attention to what they are saying, how they might be feeling, and what they might be thinking.

Take a break if you need one Finally, it is ok to take breaks during tough conversations if it feels like things are getting too heated or are no longer productive. You can just say, "I don't think we're getting anywhere with this right now, so why don't we revisit it later. I need some time."

Avoid catharsis

People often operate under the mistaken assumption that a good way to deal with unwanted anger is by "letting it out." They suggest punching a pillow, or playing aggressive sports, or even playing violent video games. In fact, over the past five to ten years, we have seen this trend of "rage rooms" opening up across the United States. Rage rooms are places where people can go and pay money to break things, and they are pitched as a way of dealing with unwanted anger.* The idea for such places is rooted in the concept of catharsis, an idea as old as Aristotle. Unfortunately, for both Aristotle and every rage room owner/ attendee, catharsis just does not work in alleviating unwanted anger. In fact, it does literally the opposite of what people want it to do.

To explain why, I want to revisit the work of Dr. Brad Bushman. He is the aggression researcher from chapter 6 where we discussed aggressive driving and a leading expert on "the catharsis myth." I interviewed him about catharsis theory and he described it like this: "Catharsis theory sounds elegant. People like it, but really there's not much scientific evidence

---

* Spoiler alert. They do not work. Also, it bothers me that they chose to call them rage rooms when there were some great puns available. Why not wreck rooms or break rooms?

to support it, so I think we need to debunk this myth that it's healthy to vent your anger or blow off steam."

He explained that while the idea dates back to Aristotle, it was revised by Dr. Sigmund Freud who described anger using a hydraulic model. "Freud argued that anger builds up inside a person like pressure inside of a pressure cooker and unless you vent the anger, the person will eventually explode in an aggressive rage. When people vent their anger, though, they're just practicing how to be more aggressive such as by hitting, kicking, screaming, and shouting. It's like using gasoline to put out a fire. It just feeds the flame."

I asked him to talk me through a study to get a sense for how we know catharsis does not work, and he told me about work he and his colleagues did where they explore catharsis within the context of the placebo effect.[55] This is one of their more recent studies, building on decades of research which finds that catharsis does not lead to decreased anger. He said, "If venting anger would work under any circumstance, it should work when people believe that it will work." So to test this out, they randomly assigned 707 participants to read either an article saying that venting worked and was healthy and providing scientific evidence to support the idea that it was a good way to reduce anger *or* to read an article saying that venting did not work, was not healthy, and providing scientific evidence to support this.

Participants then wrote a one-paragraph essay outlining their position on abortion. When they were finished, the researchers took the essay and told the participant it would be given to another participant for an evaluation (the other participant did not actually exist). Meanwhile, the participant was given an essay on abortion, purportedly written by the same "other participant," to evaluate. The essay they received was always consistent with their position so as to ensure any later aggression was not in retaliation over differences of opinion. They then graded each other's essay, with the fake participant trashing the participant's essay. As Dr. Bushman put it: "They gave them the lowest ratings possible and wrote something like 'This is the worst essay I've ever read.'" This was their anger induction.

After the participants were good and mad, they were told to either do nothing (control group) or vent their anger by punching a punching bag (experimental group). Next, they measured their anger with a mood questionnaire, and then (this is my favorite part) had participants compete with the nonexistent other participant (who they still thought was genuine) in a 25-round competitive activity where they tried to push a button faster than their opponent. When they won the game, they were allowed to punish their "partner" by playing a loud, aversive noise.* They could control how loud it was, between 0 and 105 decibels, and how long the other person had to hear it. This was their measure of aggression. When they lost the game (half the time), they received a noise blast from their "opponent" where the length and level was randomly determined

Now, if catharsis theory is true, the people who should score the lowest on the questionnaire and behave the least aggressively are the ones who (a) were led to believe catharsis would work (they read the fake article saying it was a good way to deal with anger) and (b) had the chance to punch the punching bags. However, the opposite happened. As Dr. Bushman put it, "Actually they were the most angry and the most aggressive. Not only did we not see a placebo effect, we saw an anti-placebo effect."

When you are angry, it is best to avoid these catharsis-like behaviors of "letting it out" via aggressive means – punching things, screaming and yelling, playing violent video games, watching other violent media. It does not help you deal with anger. Far from it. It is likely making the problem much worse.

---

* He played it for me over the phone, but first he described it like so: "The noise is a mixture of noises that people really hate like fingernails scratching on chalkboards, dentist's drills, blowhorns, sirens, things like that." He was right. It was awful.

Channeling anger into prosocial solutions

I am often asked when I talk about the catharsis myth: "If both suppressing and expressing anger is bad for you, what is left over?" The answer to this is actually pretty simple. Expressing your anger is not bad for you. Yes, the research has shown that expressing it in aggressive ways too often can be bad for you. But as I have said already, there are infinite ways to express our anger and many of them include channeling that frustration and rage and even fury into something positive and prosocial. So what are some of those possibilities? They are endless, but here are a few:

- **Problem solving:** Anger is alerting you to a problem. Channel your anger into identifying and solving that problem.
- **Creating art, literature, poetry, and music:** There are beautiful and powerful works of art that were both motivated by anger or serve as powerful expression of anger. Anger can be used to create meaningful and beautiful works.
- **Asserting yourself:** It is very possible (though sometimes uncomfortable) to have meaningful conversations when you are angry. Start by telling people when they have wronged you in an assertive way.
- **Seeking support:** Sometimes, when you are angry, the thing you need most is a person who will listen and hear you out, especially when the goal is less about *venting* and more about processing the frustrations.
- **Seeking broader change:** When people are angered by societal or political wrongs, they can use that anger create a better community and world – donate to or volunteer for important causes, protest wrongs, write letters to the editor, or even run for office.

ACTIVITY: USING ANGER

For this final activity, I want you to use these three steps to come up with multiple ways you personally could have used your anger in a previous situation.

1 I want you to think of a time when you were truly enraged, and even in retrospect (even after evaluating the appraisals and thoughts you had) you feel like that rage was justified.

2 Diagram just the second half of the model: What did the anger feel like in your body and what did you do with it?

3 Identify three positive, prosocial things you could have done with that anger.

Final thoughts

Even though it is associated with catharsis, I do not mind the pressure cooker metaphor of anger that underlies the idea behind catharsis. I can understand why catharsis feels accurate to people. We have likely all felt our daily frustrations build up until we explode over "something small." So I can see how it follows for people that we need to let off steam before we blow.

Instead, though, I like to think of anger differently. It is a powerful fuel that helps run the ever complicated machine that is you. And like any fuel, it can get too hot so we need to find ways to lower the temperature. That is what you are doing when you embrace relaxation or distraction. It is what you are doing when you find ways to reevaluate your thoughts or avoid cues or even make sure you stay aware of your tension states. You are finding ways to turn down the heat.

But this fuel does not need to stay cool all the time. There are times when you absolutely can and should feel anger. It is not only okay to be mad, it is sometimes right to be mad. In fact, the reason you even feel anger in the first place is because it served your ancestors so very well. It helped not just to keep them alive, but also to thrive in what was often an exceedingly difficult and cruel world. It can serve that same purpose for you now.

REFERENCES

1. Deffenbacher, J.L., Oetting, E.R., Lynch, R.S., & Morris, C.D. (1996). The expression of anger and its consequences. *Behaviour Research and Therapy, 34*, 575–590.

2. Dahlen, E.R., & Martin, R.C. (2006). Refining the anger consequences questionnaire. *Personality and Individual Differences, 41*, 1021–1031.

3. www.tmz.com/2010/11/17/bristol-palin-dancing-with-the-stars-man-shotgun-television-tv-wisconsin-steven-cowen/

4. Deffenbacher, J.L. (1996). Cognitive-behavioral approaches to anger reduction. In K.S. Dobson & K.D. Craig (Eds.), *Advances in cognitive-behavioral therapy* (pp. 31–62). Thousand Oaks, CA: Sage.

5. Foster, S.P., Smith, E.W.L., & Webster, D.G. (1999). The psychophysiological differentiation of actual, imagined, and recollected anger. *Imagination, Cognition and Personality, 18*, 189–203.

6. Lanteaume, L., Khalfa, S., Regis, J., Marquis, P., Chauvel, P., & Bartolomei, F. (2007). Emotion induction after direct intracerebral stimulations of human amygdala. *Cerebral Cortex, 17*, 1307–1313.

7. Anderson, S.W., Barrash, J., Bechara, A., & Tranel, D. (2006). Impairments of emotion and real-world complex behavior following childhood – or adult-onset damage to ventromedial

prefrontal cortex. *Journal of the International Neuropsychological Society*, *12*(2), 224–235.

Anderson, S.W., Bechara, A., Damasio, H., Tranel, D., & Damasio, A.R. (1999). Impairment of social and moral behavior related to early damage in human prefrontal cortex. *Nature Neuroscience*, *2*(11), 1032–1037.

Bechara, A., Dolan, S., Denburg, N., Hindes, A., Anderson, S.W., & Nathan, P.E. (2001). Decision-making deficits, linked to a dysfunctional ventromedial prefrontal cortex, revealed in alcohol and stimulant abusers. *Neuropsychologia*, *39*(4), 376–389.

8.   Ekman, P., et al. (1987). Universals and cultural differences in the judgments of facial expressions of emotion. *Journal of Personality and Social Psychology*, *53*(4), 712–717.

9.   Flack, W.F., Jr., Laird, J.D., & Cavallaro, L.A. (1999). Separate and combined effects of facial expressions and bodily postures on emotional feelings. *European Journal of Social Psychology*, *29*(2–3), 203–217.

10.   Martin, R.C., & Dahlen, E.R. (2007). The Angry Cognitions Scale: A new inventory for assessing cognitions in anger. *Journal of Rational-Emotive and Cognitive Behavior Therapy*, *25*, 155–173.

11.   Martin, R.C., & Dahlen, E.R., (2011). Angry thoughts and response to provocation: Validity of the Angry Cognitions Scale. *Journal of Rational-Emotive and Cognitive Behavior Therapy*, *29*, 65–76.

12.   www.detroitnews.com/story/opinion/letters/2018/07/20/open-letter-regarding-civility-public-discourse/801624002/

13.   apnews.com/1d8948d2ff4e441b94b75fe852382c7f

14.   Salerno, J.M., Peter-Hagene, L.C., & Jay, A.C.V. (2019). Women and African Americans are less influential when they express anger during group decision making. *Group Processes & Intergroup Relations*, *22*(1), 57–79.

15.   Crandall, C.S., & Eshleman, A. (2003). A justification-suppression model of the expression and experience of prejudice. *Psychological Bulletin*, *129*(3), 414–446.

16. cdn.cnn.com/cnn/2020/images/06/08/rel6a.-.race.and.2020. pdf

17. Breech, J. (2016). POLL: Majority of Americans disagree with Colin Kaepernick's protest. *CBS Sports.* www.cbssports. com/nfl/news/poll-majority-of-americans-disagree-with-colin-kaepernicks-protest/

18. Bailey, C.A., Galicia, B.E., Salinas, K.Z., Briones, M., Hugo, S., Hunter, K., & Venta, A.C. (2020). Racial/ethnic and gender disparities in anger management therapy as a probation condition. *Law and Human Behavior, 44*(1), 88–96.

19. Jacobs, D. (2017). We're sick of racism, literally. *The New York Times.* www.nytimes.com/2017/11/11/opinion/sunday/sick-of-racism-literally.html

20. Ulrich, N. (2020). NFL lifts indefinite suspension on Cleveland Browns' Myles Garrett. *USA Today.* www.usatoday. com/story/sports/nfl/browns/2020/02/12/myles-garrett-nfl-lifts-cleveland-browns-indefinite-suspension/4736004002/

21. Chuck, E. (2019). Why Myles Garrett's helmet attack likely won't result in criminal charges. *NBC News.* www.nbcnews. com/news/us-news/why-myles-garrett-s-helmet-attack-likely-won-t-result-n1083186

22. Federal Bureau of Investigation. (2018). Uniform Crime Reporting Violent Crime. ucr.fbi.gov/crime-in-the-u.s/2018/crime-in-the-u.s.-2018/topic-pages/violent-crime

23. Iadicola, P., & Shupe, A. (2013). *Violence, inequality, and human freedom.* Lanham, MD: Rowman & Littlefield Publishers, Inc.

24. Martin, R.C., & Dahlen, E.R., (2011). Angry thoughts and response to provocation: Validity of the Angry Cognitions Scale. *Journal of Rational-Emotive and Cognitive Behavior Therapy, 29,* 65–76.

25. American Psychiatric Association. (2013). *Diagnostic and statistical manual of mental disorders* (5th ed.). Washington, DC: Author.

26. Dahlen, E.R., Martin, R.C., Ragan, K., & Kuhlman, M. (2004). Boredom proneness in anger and aggression: Effects of

impulsiveness and sensation seeking. *Personality and Individual Differences, 37,* 1615–1627.

27. Dahlen, E.R., Martin, R.C., Ragan, K., & Kuhlman, M. (2005). Driving anger, sensation seeking, impulsiveness, and boredom proneness in the prediction of unsafe driving. *Accident Analysis and Prevention, 37,* 341–348.

28. Berkowitz, L., & LaPage, A. (1967). Weapons as aggression-eliciting stimuli. *Journal of Personality and Social Psychology, 7,* 202–207.

29. Tanaka-Matsumi, J. (1995). Cross-cultural perspectives on anger. In H. Kassinove (Ed.), *Anger disorders: Definition, diagnosis, and treatment.* Washington, DC: Taylor & Francis.

30. Martin, R.C., Coyier, K.R., Van Sistine, L.M., & Schroeder, K.L. (2013). Anger on the internet: The perceived value of rant-sites. *Cyberpsychology, Behavior, and Social Networking, 16,* 119–122.

31. Tippett, N., & Wolke, D. (2015). Aggression between siblings: Associations with the home environment and peer bullying. *Aggressive Behavior, 41,* 14–24.

32. Smith, T.W. (2006). Personality as risk and resilience in physical health. *Current Directions in Psychological Science, 15,* 227–231.

33. Chang, P.P., Ford, D.E., Meoni, L.A., Wang, N.Y., & Klag, M.J. (2002). Anger in young men and subsequent premature cardiovascular disease: The precursors study. *Archives of Internal Medicine, 162,* 901–906.

34. Nitkin, K. (2019). The Precursors Study: Charting a lifetime. *HUB.* hub.jhu.edu/2019/03/25/precursors-study/

35. Selye, H. (1946). The general adaptation syndrome and the diseases of adaptation. *Journal of Allergy, 17,* 241–247.

36. Musante, L., & Treiber, F. (2000). The relationship between anger-coping styles and lifestyle behavior in teenagers. *Journal of Adolescent Health, 27,* 63–68.

37. Dahlen, E.R., & Martin, R.C. (2006). Refining the Anger Consequences Questionnaire. *Personality and Individual Differences, 41*, 1021–1031.

38. Lovibond, S.H., & Lovibond, P.F. (1995). *Manual for the Depression Anxiety Stress Scales* (2nd ed.) Sydney: Psychology Foundation.

39. Martin, R.C., & Dahlen, E.R. (2006). Cognitive emotion regulation in the prediction of depression, anxiety, stress, and anger. *Personality and Individual Differences, 39*, 1249–1260.

40. Exline, J.J., Park, C.L., Smyth, J.M., & Carey, M.P. (2011). Anger toward God: Social-cognitive predictors, prevalence, and links with adjustment to bereavement and cancer. *Journal of Personality and Social Psychology, 100*, 129–148.

41. Birkley, E.L., & Eckhardt, C.I. (2018). Effects of instigation, anger, and emotion regulation on intimate partner aggression: Examination of "perfect storm" theory. *Psychology of Violence, 9*, 186–195.

42. Gilam, G., Abend, R., Gurevitch, G., Erdman, A., Baker, H., Ben-Zion, Z., & Hendler, T. (2018). Attenuating anger and aggression with neuromodulation of the vmPFC: A simultaneous tDCS-fMRI study. *Cortex, 109*, 156–170.

43. Eckhardt, C.I, & Crane, C. (2008). Effects of alcohol intoxication and aggressivity on aggressive verbalizations during anger arousal. *Aggressive Behavior, 34*, 428–436.

44. Garcia-Sancho, E., Dhont, K., Salguero, J.M., Fernandez-Berrocal, P. (2017). The personality basis of aggression: The mediating role of anger and the moderating role of emotional intelligence. *Scandinavian Journal of Psychology, 58*, 333–340.

45. Buss, D.M. (1987). Selection, evocation, and manipulation. *Journal of Personality and Social Psychology, 53*, 1214–1221.

46. Deffenbacher, J.L. (1995). Ideal treatment package for adults with anger disorders. In H. Kassinove (Ed.), *Anger disorders: Definition, diagnosis, and treatment.* Washington, DC: Taylor & Francis.

47. Schwarz, N., & Clore, G.L. (1983). Mood, misattribution,

and judgments of well-being: Informative and directive functions of affective states. *Journal of Personality and Social Psychology*, *45*, 513–523.

48. Gross, J.J. (2002). Emotion regulation: Affective, cognitive, and social consequences. *Psychophysiology*, *39*, 281–291.

49. Martin, R.C., & Dahlen, E.R. (2007). Anger response styles and reaction to provocation. *Personality and Individual Differences*, *43*, 2083–2094.

50. Linden, W., Hogan, B.E., Rutledge, T., Chawla, A., Lenz, J.W., & Leung, D. (2003). There is more to anger coping than "in" or "out." *Emotion*, *3*, 12–29.

51. Garnefski, N., Kraaij, V., & Spinhoven, P. (2001). Negative life events, cognitive emotion regulation and emotional problems. *Personality and Individual Differences*, *30*, 1311–1327.

52. Martin, R.C., & Dahlen, E.R. (2005). Cognitive emotion regulation in the prediction of depression, anxiety, stress, and anger. *Personality and Individual Differences*, *39*, 1249–1260.

53. DiGiuseppe, R., & Tafrate, R.C. (2007). *Understanding anger disorders*. New York, NY: Oxford University Press.

54. Hucke, K., & Martin, R.C. (2015). *Emotions in sports performance*. Poster presented at the Annual Midwestern Psychological Association Conference, Chicago, IL.

55. Bushman, B.J., Baumeister, R.F., & Stack, A.D. (1999). Catharsis, aggression, and persuasive influence: Self-fulfilling or self-defeating prophecies? *Journal of Personality and Social Psychology*, *76*(3), 367–376.

ACKNOWLEDGEMENTS

I am deeply indebted to many people who have supported me in writing this book. Starting with my family, I get to have my dream job because I have an incredible partner and best friend in my wife, Tina, who had faith in me before I had faith in myself. I am similarly blessed to have two amazing sons, Rhys and Tobin, who make me want to go above and beyond to help create a better world. I have a loving and extraordinarily dedicated mom, Sandy, who taught me the value of leadership and service, and a brilliant dad, Phil, who taught me to think critically and work hard. I grew up with three wonderful siblings and they, their partners, and their children have consistently been a source of love, support, and good humor. Last, I am exceedingly lucky to have inherited a similarly wonderful family in my in-laws.

There have been a number of times in my career when I have felt extraordinarily lucky for the opportunities I have received. The work I was able to do with Dr. Eric Dahlen in the Counseling Psychology program at the University of Southern Mississippi stands out as one of those times, and his support, expertise, and guidance continue to be critical to my work. Similarly, I somehow landed the perfect job in the Psychology Department at the University of Wisconsin-Green Bay, where I am surrounded by brilliant scholars and creative teachers, not just in psychology but across the university. My work as a teacher and researcher is constantly inspired by these colleagues who have been and continue to be amazing friends, co-workers, and mentors. Also at UW-Green Bay, a special thanks to my students who teach me as much as I teach them and give me hope that the world is headed in a better direction.

When it comes to opportunities I feel lucky to have had, I am so very thankful for the TEDx Fond du Lac team for selecting me to do a talk and guiding me through the process. The talents among that group are extraordinary. Finally, I am thankful for the Watkins Publishing team, especially Fiona Robertson, who supported me in writing this book. Their confidence in me and their guidance have made this possible.

I had no idea when I started studying anger more than 20 years ago how much it would intrigue me or how fulfilling this career would be. I owe so much of this joy to the brilliant scholars out there studying anger and aggression. They work tirelessly with the goal of helping people develop healthier lives, and reading their work is a constant source of inspiration.

WATKINS
1893

The story of Watkins began in 1893, when scholar of esotericism John Watkins founded our bookshop, inspired by the lament of his friend and teacher Madame Blavatsky that there was nowhere in London to buy books on mysticism, occultism or metaphysics. That moment marked the birth of Watkins, soon to become the publisher of many of the leading lights of spiritual literature, including Carl Jung, Rudolf Steiner, Alice Bailey and Chögyam Trungpa.

Today, the passion at Watkins Publishing for vigorous questioning is still resolute. Our stimulating and groundbreaking list ranges from ancient traditions and complementary medicine to the latest ideas about personal development, holistic wellbeing and consciousness exploration. We remain at the cutting edge, committed to publishing books that change lives.

DISCOVER MORE AT:
www.watkinspublishing.com

Read our blog

Watch and listen to
our authors in action

Sign up to
our mailing list

We celebrate conscious, passionate, wise and happy living.
Be part of that community by visiting

 /watkinspublishing   @watkinswisdom

 /watkinsbooks   @watkinswisdom